# the
# weaver
# &
# the
# welder

a memoir of sacred musings

by
## VICTORIA R.G. NEWBURN

THE
SELF
PUBLISHING
AGENCY

Victoria R.G. Newburn
The Weaver & The Welder

Book Design | Petya Tsankova
Editor | Kathie Lynas
Publishing Management | TSPA The Self Publishing Agency, Inc.

# WORDS OF PRAISE

"Prepare to be awakened to the world around you, the soul within you, and the web that connects us. Tori's passage through experience and intuitive wisdom is a powerhouse of words. In her first book, she shares depth of heart and spirit that is generous and profound and the balm many of us need to soothe our aching hearts."

*Katie Landry, LCSW*

"Tori is a profoundly magical, introspective being who offers her personal journey as a source of wisdom and inspiration to us all – whether we're deep down the path of spirituality or just taking our first steps."

*Justin McLeod, CEO*
*and founder of Hinge*

"*The Weaver & The Welder* is a beautiful blend of memoir, travelogue, and mystic inspiration. Tori shares her life with readers in ways that few do, in the process illuminating universal truths and encouraging readers to journey within. This book is a portal to witness Tori's gifts in full force."

*April Rinne, advisor, adventurer,*
*and author of FLUX*

"It is with utter elation and pure joy for humanity that I get to witness this divine channeling be birthed into the world. It is profoundly illuminating. Tori's powerful teachings have been timely and life changing. She is a treasure and working with her has been thrilling yet calming, deeply engaging and incredibly personal. It has been an honor. I am truly overjoyed for all who encounter its thought-provoking wisdom. What a sacred time to be alive!"

*Stephanie Simon, sister of the stars*

"*The Weaver & The Welder* is a beautiful blend of poetry and prose that unveils eternal soul codes, bringing timeless wisdom into the here and now. For the spiritual seeker, for those that explore wonder in the eternal moments of life, for those that question our purpose individually and collectively, for those that follow the Divine hand in the mystical moments, this book will awaken aspects of what you are searching for. If you want to awaken a deep and profound current of inner knowing and soulful resonance, this book is for you."

*Dr. Jill Strom, DC, CACCP, FASA,*
*and author of The Cura Connection*

"Timeless wisdom that is deeply needed in our modern times. Tori takes up the mantle of the seekers and teachers and mystics who came before her – those incredible writers who have spun deeply personal experiences into universal truths for communal healing and inspiration for all. Readers will walk away with a newly charged imprint of wisdom and a wildly more expansive and beautiful way of looking at this life and the possibilities of making a difference in our hurting world."

*Catherine Zack, author*
*and founder of Village Yoga Kinderhook*

# CONTENTS

*J, J, and R:*
*To all of the universes and back.*
*Always and always.*
*xo,*
*Mama*

# AUTHOR'S NOTE

A journal and pen rest on my bedside stand, just as they have ever since I was little. Writing poetry and jotting notes on scraps of paper are essential aspects of my creative process. Missives, musings, observations; using words to process life has always been my way.

The following pages are an expansion of these writings. After starting and restarting to write this book countless times, I have finally completed the journey. What you hold in your hands is my gift to the world. Wisdom hums within these pages for everyone, and I promise if you give it a chance, this book will give you something in return.

At the highest level, *The Weaver & The Welder* is about evolution – the transformation from one way of being into another. From a more nuanced perspective, the narrative tells the story of one woman's journey of love, loss, and the discovery of a connection to her soul. At its core, the wisdom culminates as a book about life – how both the pinnacle and mundane moments are sacred and become the threads that weave the fabric of our existence.

You might be wondering, who am I, the author and narrator of these pages? For those of you who know me, thank you for being here. To my new readers and students, also thank you for being here.

I am Tori – seeker, artist, and mystic. My other signifiers include mother, daughter, partner, sister, cousin, friend, teacher, and mentor. Most importantly, I am a human on this planet and a soul traveling the realms of being – the physical world and the dimensions beyond. Even after years of offering lectures and classes, guiding trainings, and connecting with countless students all over the world, I still feel like a student of life.

As it relates directly to the content of this book, I am intuitive and communicate with various realms and dimensions. As you will learn, my intuition and communion with my heart, soul, guides, ancestors, and the Divine current of energy that exists in all things guide many moments of my life. My purpose seeks to illuminate the path of individual and collective evolution.

*The Weaver & The Welder* offers a collection of memories and musings chronicling pivotal years in my spiritual journey. These years were transformative in both subtle and profound ways – physical, metaphysical, body, and soul. They coincided with cosmic shifts that activated my unique energetic signature. These are terms for reading the intelligence of the stars – also known as astrology. While this is not a book about astrology, I wove in key aspects of my individual cosmic design to shed light on each experience shared in these pages.

This book explores many themes: God, Divine design, the external landscape, the internal landscape, intuition, motherhood, travel, and experiences that make us undeniably human. The stories told in these pages are the anchor points along my path that guided me to unlock profound and potent wisdom. The evolution of the individual and the wisdom unveiled along the way lead to the collective evolution of humanity.

Everything written in the following pages comes from direct experience – even the moments that push the edge of reality. These memories are offered to inspire you to stay curious, to feel, to connect, to question, to contemplate, to reflect, and to trust the process of your own evolutionary journey.

These moments are raw and real, charting a path of learning how to truly pay attention, in both profound and sacred ways. Through them, I provide glimpses of vulnerability and human emotion as well as moments when my intuition expanded and unfolded in new ways. The musings integrate wisdom gathered across lifetimes and dimensions.

You may be far along the path of your own spiritual journey and individual evolution or just beginning. You might be noticing a connection to something greater: moments of déjà vu, synchronicities, or hearing the voice of your heart, soul, or guides more clearly. Perhaps this book might be your call to action. Maybe you are feeling the tug, and you simply need permission to contemplate your life and ways of being, and/or the greater ways of being.

Above all, these moments and musings are shared to guide you as you think about what is possible as it relates to our reality, time, consciousness, soul, mind, heart, thoughts, energy, intuition, body, love, family, and even your relationship with God. While the experiences are uniquely mine, the wisdom is for all of us.

Wherever you are when you find this book, know that you are exactly where you are supposed to be, and this book is now a companion on your path. May it offer a safe space to reflect on questions about life, to listen to the wisdom of your soul, and to feel the current of the Divine that flows through all. My hope is that this book becomes a familiar resting place to which you return again and again.

The title, *The Weaver & The Welder,* holds multiple meanings. It invites you to become the weaver of your life by paying attention to each moment and how they all come together to create the web of reality. The weaver embodies an awareness of the etheric currents of energy in the unseen realms that create multiple layers of experience. These layers encompass the memories and revelations of thought, the chords of the future, the electromagnetic energy of the heart, the planet and the cosmos, and the very real reality of our soul, guides, and inter-dimensional beings.

The weaver nods to evolving scientific theories – like quantum mechanics – on how our perceived reality functions. While I am no expert in this genre of scientific thought, I am a curious observer intrigued by how contemporary science seems to echo the wisdom of ancient texts. Finally, weaving is an art form that brings multiple aspects together to form a new whole – a skill that I apply in my work as a visual artist.

The invitation is also to be the welder and intentionally choose to bring together varied materials (and experiences) to create the structure of life. The welder represents how we build our lives moment to moment in this physical reality and is an archetype that embodies both strength and precision to excel in creation – honoring the physical and mental balance necessary to bring ideas into reality.

The welder is a nod to the practice of alchemy. Again, I am a curious student of the philosophy, not an expert. Alchemy is the process of merging and transforming materials to create something new and arguably more profound – for example, lead to gold. It is a philosophy rooted in the potential transformation of mind, heart, and soul. To my knowledge, the most important part of the alchemical process is evolution from one way into another, from one material into another. The alchemy of the soul is a transformation leading us to remember who we are.

Welding is also a skill I have used to create art. The act of welding allows the artist to use their hands and tools to become the creator of physical structures. It requires brawn, brain, ease, patience, and precision to build beauty and form. The welding of steel makes a joint stronger than its two individual parts and allows for the creation of objects with both purpose and beauty. Welding symbolizes how life might be if we intentionally bring parts together to make a greater whole.

A note on the use of *God*. Even though this word comforts some and triggers others, I chose it intentionally. Everyone has their own relationship with this word and an idea of what it represents. Other words used to invoke the same energy are Divine and Source. For me, they are interchangeable. I believe God is the energy at the center of everything there ever has been, everything there is, and everything there ever will be. God takes on innumerable forms, and limiting Divine energy to specific human definitions is inconsistent with the teachings – as I feel them and comprehend their true message. We cannot in these human bodies fully grasp the eternal energy of God. We can, however, feel it, and we often feel it as infinite love.

The content of this book may be simultaneously soothing and activating. Sometimes, you might feel aligned and in synch with the human stories and soulful wisdom. Other times, you might feel friction and discord. Your beliefs might be challenged, or your core values might be illuminated. If something does not resonate with you, that is okay. In fact, I invite you to use my beliefs as access points of inquiry and to feel your reactions and emotions as they arise. Give yourself space to contemplate and decide from your heart what is true to you. Maybe you are reading these pages as an opportunity to hold steadfast to what you believe – an affirmation of sorts. Or maybe, this is a moment for you to transform and evolve into new beliefs and ways of being.

As you read these memories, stories, musings, and wisdom, please know this: *to transform and evolve, we must be willing and able to change.* There are moments in life when we are willing, but we are not able, for various reasons. There are times when we are able to but not willing, for other reasons. Then there are the moments when everything aligns, and we are willing and able to continue the journey of spiritual transformation and individual evolution.

Through the evolution of the individual, the collective will one day remember that we are all holding strands of profound wisdom. When woven together, these strands create the fabric of an exquisite existence. May we build together an experience of love.

---

I invite you to take a deep breath and imagine us sitting together. Placing my left hand on my heart and right hand on my belly, I guide us through three deep breaths and recite a prayer.

If you feel comfortable, close your eyes, and repeat these phrases in your heart. Breathe and be. When you feel ready, open your eyes.

> **I am grateful for this day.**
> **I am grateful for this life.**
> **I am grateful for all things.**
> **I bow to the Divine light in all of us.**
> **Thank you as always for showing up.**

PRELUDE

# MORNING LIGHT

---

*"Get quiet enough to feel the wisdom of the heart."*
*– Intuitive Wisdom*

The sun rises over the trees to the east, illuminating the field with wonder. The deer walk calmly through the tall grasses, comfortable knowing they are safe and that this, too, is their home. The light invites my energy to drift into a reverie of contemplation.

Life is a compilation of dreamlike moments. Awareness dances between the scenes: waking and sleeping, forgetting and remembering, entertainment and revelation. In the spaces between, time morphs and transforms, shifting like the light from dawn to dusk. Countless breaths swirl with inquiry about the kaleidoscope of human experience, all while navigating the depths and density of this earthbound dimension. Our hearts forever seek connection to something greater – to soul, to ancestors, to guides, and to God.

Traversing the spaces between imagination and reality, where time finds an undulating pace rather than a linear path, for me, allows an interesting current of thought. This is the creative space where the fantasies of the internal world mix with the assumed reality of the external world. Imagination is the birthplace of human ingenuity; ephemeral ideas become the building blocks of everything in our daily lives.

And yet, for so many, this connection to the periphery of the senses, the curiosity of the heart, and the expansion of the mind seems disenchanting and disillusioned. Many prefer the ease of the known, rather than the excitement of the unknown. Quite simply, many of us have forgotten about the majestic truth of life, or we do not make time to be curious about the great mysteries.

Slowly, and soon to be quickly, we are remembering. As a collective, humanity is returning to curiosity. Looking behind the frame and seeing how the painting was hung, we are unveiling more of the mystery of being. We are discovering the nuanced architecture of the microscopic and macroscopic realities. Asking bigger questions, we arrive at even greater answers.

Magic, science, or religion, whatever name we assign to these inquiries, is finding a steady pace in our collective energy. When we expand, we invite the potential for miracles. What was once myth or fiction is becoming truth and landing into the daily rhythm of our shared reality.

As I continue gazing out the window, my thoughts weave with the morning light.

We perform the journey of seeking, both collectively and individually, under the canopy of the atmosphere of our planet. Our reality creates the stage of human experience and the perfect environment for the evolution of humanity to unfold. Everyday lives lead us through our roles as characters in the manifested world.

The play and the drama of life present us with harmonic and discordant moments that unlock the magic of aliveness. The love stories, the losses, the pining, the yearning, the seeking, all blossom into something greater than the individual parts.

Telling stories is what we humans do best. Sharing memories like a photo book – snapshots of moments lived, felt, and dreamed. Oral traditions are a living legacy. Written word becomes the artifact of times past. The overlapping interwoven narratives of the world and hopes for the future guide us collectively to an experience of wholeness and holiness. Our stories chart a map of what has been, what is, and what will be.

Watching the doe walk through the mist now rising from the warm earth and the fawn prance next to the orchard, I reflect more specifically on the stories of my spiritual journey (thus far).

My realizations and revelations were not instantaneous. Rather, through years of small shifts, I guided myself through great change.

Each of us is capable of this level of transformation. Each moment, profound or mundane, offers opportunities for evolution. Each breath becomes proof that new ways of being – believing in soul, traveling through consciousness, expanding the mind, turning inward – are possible and powerful.

Two more does join the mama and baby and I wonder about the pair of twin stags who were born last spring. My attention shifts as does the sky. The tangerine swirls mix with soft blue, pink, and white. Looking farther into the abyss above, I watch the heron fly north, indicating the dawn of a new day.

As always, my thoughts dance with the beat of evolution.

# 1

# THE CATALYST
## Devotion & Ritual

---

*"Embark into the inner realms*
*and illuminate the Divine within"*
*– Intuitive Wisdom*

Pulling the sheets closer toward my chin, I listen to the steady rain. The drips create a consonance of patterned sounds on the streets of the quiet mountain town. The lulling vibrations entice me to stay in the safety and comfort of my bed. After two weeks of travel, a certain type of exhaustion has settled into my sensitive system.

Fifteen days ago, I landed in the bustling chaos of Ho Chi Min City, the largest city in Vietnam, which is home to millions of people moving through the daily flow of life. The energy of the city was initially overwhelming, but I was eager to engage in the adventure of exploring this side of the world.

Scanning the sea of strangers at the arrivals gate, my eyes finally found a familiar smile. My cousin, who lives in the region, is my travel mate on this three-week backpacking trip and the reason I find myself in Southeast Asia. She and I could be twins: dark-brown hair, petite, unique sense of humor, squinty-eyed smile (a genetic trait shared by everyone on my father's side of the family), and an appetite for global investigation and delicious food.

Zooming motorbikes full of families and goods greeted us as we left the airport and began our navigation of this foreign place. One bike held two adults, a baby, a ladder, and a chicken, leading me to smile at the absurdity and reveal that we were complete outsiders.

Finding the courage to cross over the consistent flow of traffic was a rite of passage. If we could figure out how to get to the other side of the street, then we would receive a permission slip to stay in this dynamic place.

With eyes wide, heads spinning, and backpacks strapped to our backs, we took one small step and then many fast steps to make it across the intersection. Permission granted. This crossing was more than simply crossing the street; it was the beginning of an adventure that would guide me to a whole new level of being.

Becoming quickly obsessed with the coffee, the flavors, the fabrics, and the smiles of the people, I began unfolding into more profound layers of curiosity about time, place, belief, sacred energy, and our shared collective humanity.

Traveling from city to city, hostel to hostel, each day we merged a bit more with the multifaceted culture of land and sea and the unique cadence of life. Diving into the emerald waters, riding bikes through the flow of traffic, and floating along the river to view the majestic architecture, we found every aspect of this country to be exquisite in its own way.

Booking the ticket for this trip was an impulse and gave life to a desire to feel free and uninhibited. It was the first time I allowed for the intuitive pull and spontaneity of youth to converge. Traveling this summer is an honest attempt to satiate a certain level of wanderlust before I start my Master of Fine Arts program in the fall.

But also, something deeper resonates within me. An echo reverberates in my heart (the physical muscle at the center of my chest and the central energetic portal to my innate wisdom) reminding me of a primeval energy within.

Two years ago, I began practicing yoga to move through the grief of losing my grandmother. Through my yoga practice, a genuine curiosity about meditation, eastern philosophy, and ancient spirituality has grown steadily. Arriving to this part of the world, where the pulse still beats with imprints of times past, is in part a quest in search of this chord of resonance.

After ten days exploring the coastal culture, we arrived in the neighboring country of Laos. Choosing to settle into the quiet mountain town of Luang Prabang – home to thousands instead of millions – we began to explore a place that holds a distinctly different energy.

On our first night, we landed past dark and took the last taxi from the airport to a guest house. Banging on the door, the disheveled son of the owner welcomed us and led us to an unoccupied room toward the back. Safe and exhausted, we fell fast asleep.

The next morning, we grabbed our bags and wound our way back toward the front of the building. Greeted by many smiling faces and kind hearts, I felt a genuineness that I have never encountered. Everyone made eye contact. We felt seen and valued, and, in a sense, taken care of.

We settled our payments, apologized for the late arrival, and walked out into the day. Making our way closer to the center of town, we found another little guest house, which is where we have stayed for the last four nights. The room includes air-conditioning, an ornate wooden ceiling, a hot shower, daily clean sheets, and fresh fruit in the morning.

This rainy morning is our last full day in town. Eventually, I wrestle myself from the comfort of my bed and dress quickly in light brown pants, a white shirt, blue cardigan, and sandals. Slipping out of the room, I try not to wake my cousin. Tiptoeing down the stairs, slinging my bag over my shoulder, I pause and take a deep breath.

The dirt road is quiet as I pull my scarf closer to my neck. The rain stops, and the early-morning mountain air feels brisk in comparison to the intense heat of mid-day. We joke that the temperature here is so hot at mid-day that the only thing we can do is sit and sweat. The mornings are different – in energy and temperature.

The internal echo reverberates more as I walk in the pre-dawn light. An intuitive inkling to observe the centuries-old ritual called the Sai Bat is my inspiration to wake early. This procession is when the monks clad in bright orange fabric walk mindfully through the streets to collect alms from the community.

As I walk hurriedly to the other side of town, I see the couple we met on the plane strolling down the street hand in hand. When we chatted with them at the airport, they had mentioned that they wanted to stay long enough to truly feel the energy of the town. Pausing my steps, I hang back as to not interfere with their moment, or more specifically, I do not want them to interfere with mine.

This morning, I prefer to be alone in observation of the mindful procession.

Hearing the Sai Bat before seeing it, I feel a palpable energetic wave of ritual move through my field of awareness. Slowing my pace with reverence, I fall into line with the group of onlookers. The energy I feel while witnessing this ceremony of devotion is unique and activating. Standing quietly, I receive with my senses and feel with my heart the years of commitment, community, and connection. The details are all-consuming – the smell of incense, the gentle slow movements, the gestures of gratitude, and the willingness to trust that all sustenance will be given.

Feeling both at one with the moment and still like an outsider, I observe in silence. Another wave of awe moves through my body as I contemplate my personal relationship to this type of ritual, this embodied prayer. My thoughts flow into a reverie.

To my understanding, devotion means commitment and sacrifice, the energetic relationship formed when we return to something over and over – in good times and in bad. Ritual is the intentional creation of sacred space, repetition of actions, and specific ways of being that allow for connection and invocation.

Devotion can be an action related to any aspect of living. Ritual can be found even in the most mundane of daily tasks. Most often though, we tend to reserve these categorizations for experiences with the Divine, with God, with the religious overtones of our human existence.

Dropping into a deeper current of reflection, memories land in my mind. For most of my life, I associated the energy of ritual and devotion with a place of worship rather than a way of being – something done on Sundays or during the high holy days of the year.

While living in France, I often found myself walking up and

down the pews of small-town chapels. A pastime I chose intentionally, so that I could immerse in the energy of the quiet, unassuming spaces that mean so much to so many. In juxtaposition, I also spent hours in the grand European cathedrals that invoke a sense of majesty. As light poured in through the stained glass, the physical structures became an easy access point to call in the Divine.

When I visited the cathedral in Chartres, the Divine current was potent. On that trip, I arrived at the cathedral after dinner. The space was quiet, and the crowds from the day were gone. As I walked into the nave to experience the labyrinth on the floor, the choir started singing. This was not a performance, so I assumed it was their weekly practice. The vibrations sounded like the voices of angels.

Looking around the cathedral, my eyes absorbed mosaics, candles, and images of eternal longing, all perfectly curated to create a Divine portal on Earth. Incense burned with a sweet and earthy scent. All the details crystallized in my senses to create an elevated moment of being. Celestial inspiration was the exact quality of experience intended by the architects; gothic structures are time capsules of Divine knowing.

Feeling deeper into the memory, I imagine all the individuals who had been in those shared sacred spaces: the tears, the celebrations, the incantations, the beliefs, and the incalculable current of the Divine.

My attention draws back to the dirt road of Laos as someone bumps into me and politely apologizes. The smell of the incense – also soft and sweet – matches my memories of other sacred places. But here, in this moment, this example of embodied prayer feels completely different.

Amid the mountains, where the river splits, there have also been generations of individuals holding the highest frequency of devotion and ritual. Just like in the cathedrals and chapels of my past, the details of the Sai Bat begin to crystallize in my awareness.

Divine activation penetrates my being. A new tone and simplicity begin to rise: a rhythm and pulse that feel authentic and true, something coming from inside rather than outside. Wisdom lands with this internal song. The verses are ancient, primal, contemporary, and of the future.

The message: *God is infinite and omnipresent. Divine connection is in all things, beings, and moments. The ancient teachings and contemporary teachings alike, when received in truth, guide us to the Divine within.*

This revelation is the first note on the chord of resonance.

The next morning, the sun rises again – as it always does. Another night has passed, and a new day begins. Dressed in flowing black travel pants and a short-sleeved white shirt, we plan to deliver most of our clothes at a collection center off the main street. While we find our backpacks lighter than when we arrived, our hearts are expanded and full.

As we gather our final items from around the room, I think about the woman I met at the night market. The lines of her face told a story, and her toothless smile could light up a thousand dark nights. In our shared moment, she was a pure embodiment of presence and ease. The thought of her way of being inspires me to meditate before we check out of the guest house.

Settling into a seated posture, the sound of the waking town greets my ears. Rain falls again, and the drips off the roof serve as a metronome for this experience. Chattering thoughts of my busy internal world eventually quiet. Hypnotizing myself to the pulse of my body, I listen to the rain and the breath. Drip, drop. Inhale, exhale. Repeat. Surrendering to the physical practicality and miraculous composition of my body, I spiral evermore inward.

My awareness (thoughts and mind) moves beyond my form. No longer tethered to my body, my soul (the part of my being beyond the physical) travels my consciousness (the ineffable, multidimensional aspect of my being) and lands in the field of imagination (a dimension beyond my body). And there I stay, in the place beyond time and space, hovering above the sensations of my physicality.

Soon, my thoughts quiet completely, my imagination clears, and I transition once more toward the infinite dimension of shared consciousness, a place beyond time and space that I have never felt before. And yet, it is familiar in a soulful way.

This equanimity, this feeling of oneness, is an experience spoken about by ancient masters and contemporary teachers alike. Enlightenment – meaning to bring "light in." I feel an exuberant connection to an energy that is marvelous and majestic; simultaneously timeless, surreal, and very real. A metaphysical reality surrounds all of us and is also within all of us. Our individual and collective consciousness builds bridges connecting our individual being to the wholeness of the greater Divine being.

Albeit brief, this meditation, in a town that beats with devotion and ritual, initiates a paradigm-shifting moment on my individual path of evolution, my spiritual journey.

Mystical experiences are possible not only for the most devout, but also for the novice and every other being willing to show up with curiosity and receptivity.

My meditation is the second note on the chord of resonance.

My eyes open as I gasp with breath. Still aware of the shared field of consciousness, my brain processes, my body receives, and my heart believes.

Then suddenly, like a flush of water moving through my being, my intuition (what feels like a memory without the experience to contextualize the thoughts) activates. A voice that is my own, yet sounds different in tone and information, reverberates through my whole being. It shares a direct and clear premonition of my journey ahead. The vision shows me my work in the world, my family, and my path – should I choose to accept it.

Breathing deeply, I am awestruck and inspired, glowing, and wrapped in the harmony of being. Feeling into the years upon years of generations of humans doing this same practice in this place, this portal, I wonder how many souls have experienced something similar and how many more will arrive at this place seeking connection, truth, comprehension, anything, and everything.

This is the third note on the chord of resonance.

For a few more moments, I steep in these revelations, the bolt of intuition, and the harmonious chord of resonance to something greater. A thought drifts in about a book I read prior to the trip and ignites another layer of inner knowing.

In the book, the protagonist unveiled portals to other dimensions. Realms that only reveal themselves after the individual reaches a certain frequency and becomes the energetic match necessary to drop the illusions. Trying to imagine the immaculate energy of such a place and such a way of being, I believe in my heart that one day, in one lifetime, I will achieve that level of holiness in human form.

As is true for every hero, there is a catalyst – the moment when the first veil drops. My catalyst, a call from my heart and an invitation from my soul (the energetic aspect of my being that transcends time, space, and travels lifetimes and dimensions) is happening here and now. The mystical is reality, and my perspective and perception begin their metamorphosis.

The world we live in is a multidimensional (meaning dimensions beyond what we perceive with our senses) realm of infinite potential, where we co-create reality, weave the timelines, and build the bridges between the portals of possibility.

Spiraling inward, we connect to the heart, the voice of the soul. Spiraling outward, we connect to the shared pulse of humanity. Spiraling above, we connect to the shared consciousness. And spiraling below, we connect to the Earth consciousness. Spiraling evermore inward, we connect to the chord of resonance within.

Standing up, I grab my backpack. Glancing one more time around the room, I take a deep breath of gratitude and walk out toward the pulsing town. With each breath, I evolve.

## unknown becomes known

here in this life
we are guests
and we are hosts

we are the dreams
memories and thoughts
of the planet on which we walk

following the collective metronome of the day
existing among a home to so many
paths converge in a medley of prophecy and chance

whether we are aware of it or not
energy is shared
and absorbed

expressions of thought
and the blossoming of a bud
are the same explosion of being

humans are magnetic
world-changing
and reality-shifting

in comprehending
the subtleties of experience
the unknown becomes known

complexities that were once beyond our cognition
enliven every aspect of existence
we are forever in a cycle of giving and receiving

# 2

# JOIE DE VIVRE

## Abundance & Joy

---

*"The illuminated soul rises.*
*Embrace the experience of being.*
*Receive the abundance of each breath."*
*— Intuitive Wisdom*

Baking bread must be somewhere close. The scent lofts its way toward my table as I take a sip of espresso. Mixed with diesel fumes and crisp morning air, the smell is unmistakably French.

A man walks by with a cigarette in his mouth and his hands behind his back. Wearing an old coat the color of light-brown fur, he moves with a nonchalant cadence – existing in a world all to himself. The streets get busier as the city starts its day. A sweetness guides this way of life. Familiar and calming, this slow way of being suits me.

In this exact moment, the entire world seems to be blooming. Moving unhurriedly through the ancient streets gives me a chance to take it all in. Paris in the springtime is wholly different than the biting winds of winter. A vitality comes with the reemergence after the long nights. More levity guides the steps when the air turns warm, and the sun stays for a longer daily promenade.

In the South of France, the lavender is already growing taller, and the blossoms on the first poppies are screaming, "I am alive; I am alive." Aliveness is the energy of each moment.

Stopping to look at petals on the cherry trees, I think about the time he and I were in the city together. Just the two of us moving through the streets with naive abandon. Cheeky Americans chasing the lights of the Eiffel Tower. Strolling arm in arm pretending to be so much to each other and already being so much to each other. Knowing that somewhere on some timeline we would eventually find our way back to each other.

Back then, almost six years ago, we were just friends. Now, it feels like something has shifted – an awakening bond between us. Even though we are still living our independent lives, him in Boston, me in Washington, D.C., our communication has increased. We seem more drawn to each other than ever before. Just days ago, before I boarded my plane, I sent him a message inviting him to come with me, to join me on this trip.

He said, "No, not this time."

My eyes close, drifting further into my imagination, where I conjure an image of him next to me to feel his strength and ease. Remembering how I felt during dinner that late autumn day in the North End of Boston, when we were roommates, brings heat to my cheeks and a smile to my lips.

In the memory of that day, four years ago, he wore a tailored jacket and wool scarf wrapped around his neck. His striking, cobalt eyes matched a perfectly groomed blonde beard – making him look distinguished. We spent the afternoon hours poring over old texts and poetry at a used bookstore. Feeling hunger rise, we found our way to a small Italian restaurant and sat at a table in the back. He ordered the wine, I ordered the lamb, and we toasted for hours.

Holding each other's gaze longer than friends might, we felt a soulful knowing of the role we each play in our shared story. The whole scene was like a moment from a movie.

Steeping in the memory, these thoughts cause something to flutter in the center of my chest: an energy in my heart, a bolt up and down my spine, like something coming alive within.

And yet, there is a reason I am here alone. A piece of me asks to unfold of its own accord, navigating the path of finding my highest expression, just like the blossoms of the cherry trees opening toward the rays of creation. A knowing of self rises before my hand reaches for the mirroring match in the external world.

When I look at the blossoms of a cherry tree, I see the petals are a soft pink, with each petal similar in hue, forming an imprint of color on my eyes. On closer investigation, I perceive that every petal differs in shade and detail. Each opening at the perfect moment and holding its unique aspect among the mass of blooms.

The same goes for humanity. We all live on this shared planet, in our co-created reality. And yet, everyone experiences their own version, expressing in their own way when the combination of inputs becomes exactly right. The space between moments is where we merge, overlap, and share in the wonder of this human experience. The present (the now) is where we find the potential of all there is – living the stories of our lives, moment by moment.

The cornucopia of being offers much to experience. It invites immense awe about the complexity of our world and the abundance of life. There are simply no two beings who hold the same energetic makeup or who embody the same physical vessel. All of us seek answers, desire matched frequencies, and push to create more and be more. A network of life on and in a planet that herself holds a unique and necessary signature among the cosmic family. Each planet and star plays their own role in the building and forming of the whole of the solar system and the multiverse beyond.

As my thoughts continue to flow, I stop in my tracks and look up; the brightness of our star – our sun – creates an almost blinding glare. The light that gives life is in this moment consuming every part of my being with intentional touch and respect. Consenting to this dynamic relationship of light and life, I open to receive.

This life, this magical, majestic life is a bustling mass of beings: the colors, the vibrancy, the exchange of humanness, holding on, letting go, giving, and receiving. Figments of reality merge at one juncture to create a point on the grid of being. Everything is energy – moving, growing, living, and dying – repeating the cycles of existing. The beings on this planet engage in a constant state of emerging, like the blossoms of spring.

A musing flutters to the forefront of my mind: "Maybe none of it is real. Maybe it all is. Maybe it is the essence of nothing and everything all at once?"

As I ponder these thoughts, my feet begin taking me toward the Saturday market in the heart of Paris. There is a rhythm to this walk – a routine that is almost automatic. The market provides a dependable meeting place in our rapidly changing world. It hosts a similar experience week after week, with different offerings depending on the season – a nurturing aspect of community. Strolling up and down the stalls, I do not recognize anyone, and yet the smells and sounds are timeless and familiar.

My eyes land on a green jade ring – a simple band, like a wedding ring – displayed on black velvet, and I decide to buy it. Handing the coins to the seller, I look them in the eyes and smile. Placing the ring on my left ring finger with a smirk, I indulge in a brief foreshadowing that flashes in my mind. Not knowing when, I see a premonition of the day when a ring is offered to me as a sign of love and commitment.

Quickly, I switch the jade ring from my left hand and place it on my right as I stuff my hands into the pockets of my gray linen shorts. Releasing one hand, I adjust my scarf and straighten the front of my black blazer as I meander through the stalls and chatter of life.

Walking by the grand church a few blocks away from the market, a familiar tingle of intuition moves through my body. My thoughts again drift away from the material world.

My internal murmurings swirl into future manifestations of home and partner. The fact that my family is gathering in France to celebrate my sister and her soon-to-be husband sharing their vows gives rise to the inspiration for these thoughts. Projecting my mind into a few days from now, I think about her white dress, the eagerness and trust they have in each other, their love and commitment. Part of me so deeply wants him, my dearest friend, to be here; it feels like he belongs at this family celebration.

Turning the corner, I decide to sit at a small café and order another espresso and croissant. Using my Parisienne accent rather than the Provençal tone that became natural when I lived in the South, my French can pass as almost fluent. Watching the men across the café and listening a bit to their conversation, I feel amused and inspired by my ability to comprehend their voices. Just minutes ago, someone asked me for directions, and I shared the way. Paris has felt comfortable since my first trip when I was eleven years old.

That summer, so many years ago, I stayed in the 11th arrondissement and spent weekends outside the city picking cherries from the trees. A highlight from those weeks in Paris was tasting my first pain-au-chocolate. The whole trip was life-changing – in more ways than just the pastries. Returning many years later to live and study during a semester in college had felt like a homecoming. Something about the energy of this country resonates with my core. Each region is distinct in its own culture, and yet a harmonic way of being flows throughout – the joie de vivre.

Reaching into my bag, I retrieve my journal and pen and start to write. A banging sound above me draws my attention to a woman shaking out a rug over her balcony. She smiles and waves to a friend walking below. Shifting my attention back to the page and my own thoughts, a truth pours into my being – messages from beyond time and space. Receiving, rather than resisting, I open myself to the reverie and channel my intuition through the practice of writing – easy and natural, just as the planet receives the light of the sun.

The words synchronize with my breath, creating a deep current of knowing. Daily intentional acts – like walking the streets with gentleness and ease or writing thoughts onto pages – consciously move energy through the world. When done with focus and attention, these acts activate joy. Allowing movement and musings to inspire the heart becomes a practice, a way of being that embodies the abundance of life. Focusing inward, while also appreciating the beauty surrounding, opens channels to elevated self-expression and wisdom from a higher aspect of soul.

When we do things that make us happy, we feel happy. We activate an appreciation for life. This continues to cultivate our relationship with abundance. Conversely, we can choose to live in fear and lack, which is the choice of scarcity. Scarcity keeps us grasping, incomplete, and chasing ideals of what could be or should be.

Choosing the energy of abundance gives us permission to unfold and soften in all the moments – to know there is enough – whatever is there, it is enough. The practice of abundance cultivates trust in the truth that the Divine will provide all that we need, even when we cannot see the full picture.

Pausing for a moment, I breathe deeply. Scents of other fresh-baked pastries drift from the boulangerie across the street. Sounds of joviality come from a group of youthful beings under the trees. They remind me of friends from the art school I attended during my college semester in Provence. Smiling at the nostalgia, I wave to the garçon at the café for the bill and exchange coins and gratitude. Returning my notebook to my bag, my reverie continues as I walk toward the banks of the Seine.

These thoughts, my thoughts that span time and space, that travel dimensions and peek to the edge of reality and back, serve as some of my greatest companions. Intentionally getting lost in order to find my way – through the musings, through the streets. Eventually orienting myself, I know exactly where I am – physically and metaphysically.

My stroll continues as I head toward Place des Vosges. This famous square holds many memories. The memory of when he and I walked together as it rained over the Seine so many years ago, ignites in my heart. Swirling in this bouquet of emotion, I remain absorbed in his energy and indulge in how I felt when he greeted me at the Gare du Nord, one of the railway stations in Paris where the Train à Grande Vitesse (TGV) arrives and departs. Sweeping me off my feet in one of those full body embraces, spinning me around with excitement, he smiled at me with such joy and kindness.

My memory focuses on the subtle creases of his eyes that appear when he is genuinely happy and at ease. Staying in this place of my mind a bit longer, I reflect on the way we make each other laugh. Our shared energy is familiar, safe, and secure. Another smile moves across my face. These memories remind me of what it feels like to be in the true resonance of joy.

The sounds of laughter from another group of friends enjoying a walk along the square bring me back to the present moment, to my breath, to here and now. My thoughts continue to shift and expand as I walk along the store fronts and watch families picnic on the grass.

Enjoyment – the act of bringing joy into physical form. Contentment – the feeling of ease and satisfaction. The enjoyment of life is necessary. True codes of enjoyment attune us to an intentional relationship with abundance. This relationship builds a bridge to something bigger. Believing in something beyond the individual that cannot be fully comprehended or even touched is a practice that allows each of us to experience the truth of aliveness and the beauty of being human. Belief then nurtures a connection with Source energy, and in turn, a connection to the multiverse, to soul, to the Divine – to the God of many names.

Inviting contentment into our energetic field guides us to cultivate the wisdom that we exist as an essential part of the greater whole. In this recognition of communion, rather than separation, we feel that life means something, even amid the occasional ugliness of the world.

We each bring breath into a unique set of lungs and return the molecules back to the collective atmosphere of air circulating the planet – transformed slightly by our individual signature. We drink water and give it memories, which goes back down to the Earth, carrying with it our energy. We activate grid lines as we walk on the Earth. Each moment, we knowingly or unknowingly infuse our imprint and ways of being into the matrix of energy that creates this reality. These energetic footprints merge throughout the millennia; from the very first of us to the very last, we are all connected.

Each of us plays a role, an essential role. A role that is ours and only ours. A role that moves the narrative, shifts the narrative, rewrites the narrative. A role that sometimes, for a moment, holds the narrative in a sacred pause of respect and wonder. The intention of the individual transforms the collective whole.

Joy allows our energy to support the omnipresent current of global coherence – a potential elevated way of being. Joy guides our individual heart to synch with the collective of hearts. Yes, our hearts ache when we see images of suffering. And yes, our hearts soar when we see images of laughter, kindness, companionship, and ease of being.

To know joy is the right of everyone on this planet. The path of igniting this aspect of self requires immense attention and commitment. A practice of intention requires conscious consumption of all that comes into our senses (sight, sound, taste, smell, and touch). When we truly feel joy and contentment, we connect – to all things, all beings, to the planet, and the cosmos.

What if, like the marketplace, we each find our own piece of this Earth where we offer our gifts? A temporary declaration of existence created to share our abundance. What if we all chose to gather at one long table and share a feast? What joy this would create – the laughter, the union, the connection. In this communion, we might finally remember that life is the dream of the Source of being. And in that dream, anything is possible.

We are a beautiful, evolving menagerie of beings striving for the fullest expression of what it means to be human. When we source from within – tapping into the infinite energy of God existing at the center of all things everywhere – we remember that there is always enough.

Walking back across the river, I glance down Île de la Cité, in awe of the gothic structure of Notre-Dame. Trying to avoid the crowds, I wander through the neighborhoods. Eventually, I find my way to my favorite place in the city and stop at a bench in front of the fountain at Jardin du Luxembourg.

Children set boats in the water and watch them float, with blue and red sails going this way and that. A small boy runs up to me and tries to hand me a boat. Speaking to him in simple French, he giggles back.

Smiling, he runs away as his mother calls to him, "Allons-y, chéri."

Surrounded by the scenes of life, I notice a family sharing a bushel of bananas and hear more sounds of laughter. A woman holds the arm of a friend. Their shared energy indicates that they have known each other forever. They smile and walk slowly with such grace. A relaxing wave moves through the center of my chest – the joy of living.

Casting my gaze once again upward to the cerulean blue of the sky and the light of our sun, I relish in all of it: the sights, the smells, the sounds, the texture, and the taste. A peculiar sensation that I am being watched causes me to glance over my shoulder. Part of me hopes it is his eyes watching; I have a sense of him being here and sharing this moment. As I smile at a stranger, I realize it is not. Not now. Now is not yet our time.

Maybe this feeling was another premonition of a future moment overlapping and weaving into this present moment. Settling into myself, into my abundance, perception, intentions, intuition, and capacity to receive what is directly here, directly now, I enjoy a deep breath.

My watch ticks and I realize that I need to make my way back toward the hotel and then to the train station. In a few hours, I head to Provence: south to more familiar towns and landscapes, to the celebration of marriage, love, and flowing white fabric. South to the embrace of family, to even more contentment, and joy. Onward evermore to the evolving reality of what life is becoming.

Here, though, this moment is for me. Alone on a bench in Paris, I feel an extremely potent sense of ease. A feeling of joy, a contentment, and way of being because I am alone. Just me and my thoughts in the city that has meant so much to me for so many years – like an old friend strolling arm in arm.

Taking another deep breath, I close my eyes and feel the sun on my face. All is well. All is right.

## ignite within

we move and breathe
the intricacies of our bodies
maintain a steadiness

we think we need to do so much
our thoughts are funny like that
convincing us of things that are not true

life is simple really
innate curiosity keeps us growing
evolving and remembering

each moment we have an opportunity
to notice the expression of life
the truth of here and now

the beings on this planet
are vast and complex
we share a rhythm and pulse

when not interrupted
life flows with ease
and invites us to ignite within

beauty, presence, and stillness
we are here to embody
joy, gratitude, and love

# 3

# MULTIPLE TRUTHS AT ONCE

## Awareness & Transformation

---

*"In the collective sea of change,*
*one small shift leads to more awareness.*
*Awareness evolves consciousness.*
*Consciousness connects all realities."*
*– Intuitive Wisdom*

After hours of thrashing in the sheets, my exhausted mind makes me irritable. Though nothing is ostensibly wrong, I mope about the cabin in a melancholy mood. My agitation is more nuanced. The inner purr of my awakening heart desires something new alongside my deepening practice of awareness – truly learning to pay attention. Though all it finds are old patterns of being.

Clanging pans louder than necessary while doing the dishes, misplacing my coffee more than once, I find the cabin starts to feel claustrophobic. My sister, her now husband, my mom, and dad are trying to enjoy the morning amid my outbursts. Fairly seasoned with my moods, they all have their approaches when I am in this state. Right now, they are simply trying their best to enjoy a calm morning at the lake.

We have been up at the cabin for almost a week. Every year, we make this pilgrimage to an isolated old fishing village that has been upgraded enough to host some modern comforts, creating an idyllic ambiance but not too fancy. The cabins are simple. Scratchy sheets and old plaid bedspreads are part of the charm. The taxidermal fish that hang from the walls of the lodge have been giving us the same looks for years.

Something about this lake is majestic – miles and miles of North Woods wilderness. Loons, herons, eagles, snakes, frogs, fish, deer, and porcupines have all been spotted throughout the years. A few summers back, a lone wolf was tracked in the woods. We were encouraged to pay attention at night, and if we listened carefully, we might hear the howl. Our family tales include the infamous story of my sister being spooked by a bear who was rummaging through the garbage. We still do not know who was more scared, my sister or the bear.

Amplifying the familiarity and welcoming energy of this place, thirty-plus family members and friends make the same journey, the same week, every year. Our North Woods excursion is special in the most precious of ways. Here on this lake, with these family members and friends, I feel infinitely safe, loved, and connected.

Amid the energy of family reunion and frivolity, this annual week holds space as a retreat – from life, expectations, and responsibilities. The natural wonder, beauty, and comfort drop me into a necessary reset. Time between the crystal-clear waters and towering pines allows me to think more clearly. Every year, toward the end of the week, I find myself in a space of renewal and revelation. Days here are like waking moments peeking into the dream of life, the truth of existence.

As I continue to clatter pots between exasperated sighs, my dad does not comment on my mood. Instead, he offers to take me on a canoe ride and get out of the cabin for a bit. When I agree, the other three share a collective sigh of relief.

For long moments, we glide quietly across the water, occasionally commenting on the stillness of the lake and the overcast sky. Cautiously, my dad embarks on a more serious conversation. He matches my tone of curiosity, intelligence, and wisdom. We often find ourselves in discourse about religion, prayer, purpose, and food recipes.

Today, he inquires about how I am really feeling. Noticing his attempt to right my energy and discontinuous thoughts, I offer a semblance of a response and soften with a listening ear. He gently recommends that I look at life from all angles, as every good daughter of a lawyer knows how to do.

"Many moments in life provide us experiences we cannot fully comprehend," he says. "In time, it all begins to make sense. Try to see it from a new perspective."

A noticeable shift of energy in my being arrives as we talk about viewpoints, opinions, and the practice of releasing the need to always be right or perfect. He focuses his advice on letting go. As we both paddle, I listen more intently to what he is saying.

Shifting perspective anoints us with the capacity to receive all experiences as an opportunity to grow. Elevating our awareness guides us to transition from critical viewpoints of judgement into acceptance. We learn that all moments have purpose and sometimes even levity. Feeling the intensity of a situation and choosing to move forward with a new perspective requires patience and practice. Not identifying or attaching, simply feeling what is actually happening. Learning to let go of things, relationships, and ways of being that no longer serve our growth creates space for transformation. These are vast and lifelong lessons.

The practice of awareness leads us to appreciate the incomprehensible beauty of each and every moment.

Suddenly, my dad and I find ourselves upside down in a group of lily pads. In a perfect moment of us both moving to look at something in the same direction, our shared weight tilted the canoe, and splat – into the water we went. Drenched, waist-deep in mucky lake water, and alongside an upside-down canoe, we hysterically laugh at the ridiculousness of the situation.

My dad has one of those laughs that consumes his whole body. When his spirits are high, he embodies a jolliness usually reserved for a character in a children's book. Right now, standing in the shallow part of the lake, he laughs so hard tears begin to roll down his cheeks.

With the dragonflies and horseflies buzzing around our heads, we try to right the canoe and slip back in, hoping no one will notice. And then we hear it, the applause of our family – siblings, aunts, uncles, and cousins – hooting and hollering from the dock at the entertaining scene. We again start laughing – so hard we barely keep the boat steady.

Earlier iterations of me would have been riddled with embarrassment. Now, in this current version, I feel the humor and frivolity. Everything is relative in the greater cycles of being.

Moments when laughter is the most appropriate reaction are ripe for the practice of awareness. More specifically, the practice of impermanence. Holding elevated awareness allows us to recognize the temporary reality of all things. We laugh because it is fleeting. We laugh because we know the moment will not last forever. We laugh because sometimes the human experience is absurd and beautiful at the same time. Just like all things, good or bad, the laughter, too, eventually ends. With awareness, we fully absorb each moment as it arrives.

Finally flipping the canoe, we climb back into the hull and paddle, sopping wet, back to the dock. Trudging to the cabin to peel off my wet sweatshirt and jeans, I collapse on my bed. Releasing a sigh and a small laugh, I shake my head at the hilarity of this situation and the hilarity of this life.

Nothing lasts forever. Savor what is and prepare for what will be. Rather than resist the growing pains of life and the embarrassing situations, receive the beauty of life with each breath. These nuggets of wisdom ease into my mind.

Emergence from melancholic ways of being becomes possible when we embrace our fleeting human experiences. All of life is temporary. Learning how to hold this elevated awareness can take lifetimes. Finding guides along the path in the form of family, friends, and even strangers, helps us to embrace multiple perspectives, transmute what we think we know, and unveil new ways of being.

Then, we move through the world giving and receiving, engaging in community rather than isolation, believing in collaboration rather than competition, and intentionally choosing to trust the flow of life. Our momentary truth of being makes more sense as each experience leads to the next. Even when we experience vulnerability, elevated awareness guides us to hold the higher perspective.

The gray, overcast sky transitions to a steady rain. My family and other members of the village go into town for groceries, gas, and a stroll through the odd shops that line the old logging junction. The town, still miles from the fishing village, does not have a stoplight. In the past few years, though, someone opened a coffee shop on the main street. It is a lovely spot to pass a rainy afternoon, where my sister and cousins settle in for a cup of something hot and lively conversation. Alone in the cabin, and happy to be, my thoughts continue.

Transformation is not monotone or monochromatic. Each of us decides how, why, and where we show up for ourselves and for others. None of us evolve in the same way. Even siblings growing up in the same environment become completely unique people. The similarities and/or differences may cause friction or an opportunity to recognize the potential of each individual.

One of the more difficult lessons to integrate is that while we actively choose to transform and evolve ourselves, we cannot change other people. Shifting the way we are, the way we react, and the way we move through the world is an individual choice to make. Once we embody a new level of awareness, our ways of being will show the maturation and, in turn, potentially become inspiration for others. Individual agency remains paramount.

Elevated awareness requires the capacity to hold multiple truths at once. If one person needs something and another needs something different, they can have these things and still coexist. Two opposing belief systems can represent truth to different people. We might evolve along different paths from the ones we love, and yet our shared experiences and connection points will strengthen our bonds. Everyone has the power and the right to evolve or stay the same, based upon what they are willing and able to endure. Awareness is the key to unlocking the energy of our shared potential and innate wisdom of the heart.

The sound of the shower immediately eases the chill settling into my body. Standing longer than necessary in the comfort and warmth cascading over my form, I indulge in my senses, which lull me into a deeper moment of reflection.

Another level of awareness exists beyond the perception of the five senses and the current moment. The awareness of the heart synthesizes multiple streams of input from multiple dimensions. Constantly communicating with the shared field of energy, the heart feels before the brain processes. Individual heart energy becomes a data stream informing the collective. Clarifying this data stream is a practice that requires each of us to align with our fullest expression, and, in turn, the fullest expression of humanity.

Coming back from my thoughts into the now moment, I turn the shower handle to the off position and take a deep breath. The towel feels gentle as I pat the warm water from my body. The softness of my sweatshirt is equally comforting on my now-dry skin. Snuggling into the chair by the window, I begin holding a personal vigil of silence while staring at the lake.

The afternoon drips by as I transition from thought to writing while continuing to glance toward the rain-kissed water. A loon swims by and the pair of eagles fly overhead. The ripples on the surface hold their own frequency of impermanence.

Eventually, the rain stops, and I decide to again go out onto the lake. This time in the rowboat. A choice that offers a bit more stability and a rhythmic soundtrack of creaky oars. Rowing far toward the other side, layers of awareness unlock and unfold. Something feels immensely uncomfortable and at the same time enticing.

As I allow for and invite in the energy of growth and transformation, immense waves of revelation roar through my being. Calling me to take off the masks and truly get to know myself, learn to love myself, and believe in my path of becoming. Blossoming awareness guides me to believe in my greater potential and to try to find the courage to claim it.

Speaking aloud to the water, wind, and sky above, "I want to live a life fully aware, awake, and alive … illuminating myself and the world with authentic truth."

And then it comes, a waterfall of tears, flowing like the warmth of the shower I felt hours ago. My declaration released something within – like a valve that was rusted shut finally succumbed to the pressure of the other side. Cracked wide open, I weep on the waters of reflection. Just me, the rowboat, and the animals of the woods who tend not to be bothered by the fragility of the human experience.

Crying and crying and crying, not about any one thing, but crying about everything: the pain and joy, the stagnation and movement, the discomfort and liberation, the oppositional reality of this life. Exploring my wonderment of the human capacity to feel the aching and the love – all of it – I pause in awe as tears roll down my cheeks.

Transformation is the courage to let go, the discomfort of growth, and the thrill of the unknown all woven together. It requires the breaking of hearts open and wide and the welding of the pieces back together.

The individual willing to transform holds the greatest power to influence collective evolution. Like the caterpillar in its chrysalis or a newborn emerging from the womb, transformation is messy, yet profound. It demands a willingness to journey, to surrender, and to uncover new realms and sacred connections. A pulse calls us inward and onward, deepening our relationship with ourselves, each other, and the planet.

These emotions are such an extreme juxtaposition to the way I felt in Paris. Just a few months ago, I was alone, blissfully walking in the spring sun, embracing thoughts of him, of the future, and feeling profound contentment and ease. Now, I am alone in the caverns of my individual being, awakening to my own potential, unsure of where I am going, and learning to trust in my path. Swaying with the eternal ebbs and flows is a natural part of the practice of being.

And then another revelation hits me with what feels like cold water in the face: *for years, my heart has been on this spiritual journey, following the hum of a song that weaves its melody from deep inside.* Harmonious internal chords inspire me to know more, to investigate, and to lift the veil. Yearning, curious, desiring to uncover the mysteries, and wanting to evolve, my soul too has always been on this trajectory – lifetime after lifetime after lifetime. My heart and soul co-create my lived experiences in order to evolve.

Here and now, I intentionally choose to unlock more insightful

levels of awareness. Even in the discomfort, my unfolding awareness inspires me to continue pursuing more profound paths of my
spiritual journey and diving evermore into the "why" and the "what"
of life.

Just like the laughter, my tears are also temporary. Feeling my
shoulders relax, I drop into the weight of my body sitting on the cold,
flat bench of the boat. The clouds part and rays of summer sun peak
through, creating what looks like a fan of light-codes in the sky. Re-
positioning a seat cushion behind my head, I lay my now exhausted
body down.

As relaxing energy flows through, my body drifts between levels of consciousness – so close to sleep and also engaging with my
thoughts. Navigating toward an internal space of my heart, I listen
to the waves lapping against the aluminum hull and travel further
into my meditation.

One of my teachers recently guided us to visualize the heart as
a cave.

"Within the cave," she said, "You will find a being. This being
will be full of light. Seated in a peaceful way. Neither here nor there.
Simply existing in pure radiance. Go to this being and sit with them."

She went on to explain, "This being is a part of you – an aspect
of your soul. It is the guardian of the heart, which is a portal to Divine wisdom. This being resides within you for many reasons. Go to
this being as often as possible. Sit with them and receive. They hold
the answers to the questions you are too afraid to speak aloud."

After these instructions, she held space for more than twenty
minutes of meditation. Following her guidance with the exactitude
of a student desiring to know more, gain more, and see more of the
mystical truth of this world, I was not disappointed. The clarity of
the vision, the familiarity of the being, and the release of energy felt
potent and real.

In that moment of meditation, a knowing blossomed from within. With it, I received a profound awareness that we are never alone,
we are infinitely wise, and there is so much more to this life. Awe-
struck by the recognition that the vastness of the cosmos and multiple dimensional realities exist within our own hearts, I realized that

we are all here on purpose and with purpose – guided and protected.

Here on the lake, I return in my mind to this cave, to the wisdom of this being, the guardian of my heart, and I ask: "What now, what am I supposed to do now?"

The answer quietly comes in my own voice, "Trust and breathe. Be brave, be strong, be powerful. You know exactly what you came here to do. Remember."

A wave of ease begins to wash over me; my emerging level of awareness is the stimulus. The veils of doubt and agitation drop as I elevate toward a higher expression.

New awareness flows through my being as wisdom lands. Accept the temporary reality of all things; remember our multidimensional reality; multiple truths exist at once; embrace profound feeling. All these teachings mix with the desire to pay attention to every detail of this human life and embrace each experience as a moment of highly concentrated energy, brilliantly beautiful in its perfection.

Squinting into the sun, I sit up and steady my body. Looking around in wonder of this landscape, I notice a family of otters playing close to the shoreline. A ping hits my chest as I ponder all that has transpired since I first misplaced my coffee in the early hours of this morning. Reaching for the oars, I begin to row. Pausing for a moment to feel the breeze coming off the water, a new reverie, which feels fresh and vibrant, arrives in my mind.

This particular movement of air, the winds of these woods, the smell of these trees, and the sounds of the water link me to all the times I have floated on this lake and all the times I will return to this reflective portal of knowing.

Air becomes breath. The same air is being breathed by everything living on the surface of this Earth. The atmosphere holds the perfect amount of oxygen to sustain the billions of humans and innumerable other beings sharing this planet. The cycle of plants and water creates this oxygen. Water droplets move all the way from the glacial lake, through the trickling creek, eventually returning to the vast ocean. One day, I know, I too will make my way to the same vast ocean.

Right now, though, ease continues to wash over me. Steeping

in the awareness of all there is, I feel the potency of now. Everything exists in the primal vibration of being.

Slowly and steadily, I row my way across the lake – toward the cabin, toward my family, my community, and evermore toward the embodiment of the momentary evolution of being. A bit of laughter rises in my chest as I smile and shake my head.

"Oh, this human life, what a ride."

## incredible realms of being

step fully into the heart
activate transcendent capacities
feel what it means to be an agent of insight

an immense amount of awareness
is required to notice
the almost inconceivable moments of being

believing before seeing
becomes
essential

believing before feeling
elevates
our awareness

transformation builds a foundation
create portals to the unseen network of our souls
our brains alone cannot compute

show up fully
embrace the formless
just as we do the form

incredible realms of being
are waiting patiently
in the place of infinite awareness

# 4

# THE SPACE BETWEEN
## Seeking & Humanity

---

*"Humanity is an aspect of a conscious planetary being orbiting a star.*
*Between that star and the planet is the experience of being alive.*
*Seek the magic in every moment."*
*– Intuitive Wisdom*

The sky is dark as the wheels hit the tarmac. Landing in Denpasar, the capital of Bali, in Indonesia, I am immensely curious. Signs in the airport guide me through the transition from plane, to bathroom, to customs, and eventually to the exit. Traveling with just my backpack makes this process light and easy.

Immediate relief floods my system as I step through the doors and feel the warm breeze brush my face. While I am an experienced traveler, twenty-plus hours of cramped quarters will make anyone crave fresh island air.

Here on a whim and with encouragement from my mentor, the trip is indeed spontaneous. Much in my life has shifted and wanderlust has again attracted my attention. The impulse to book the trip was similar to the feeling I had when I decided to travel to Vietnam and Laos. Following a call, not in a physical sense, but rather listening to the ever-increasing chords of the song of the heart, calling me inward.

Friends and fellow teachers told me about the ancient knowing woven into this island. They were right. The vibrations of sacred energy infuse my being the moment my feet touch the ground. Patient, rhythmic, humming energy creates an almost immediate transformation. A gentle beauty and distilled way of being exists through connection with elemental energy, Divine design, and to God.

Crowds of loud, bustling travelers gather next to lines of taxis. A stranger with a gentle smile holds a sign with my name. He appears older, wise even. He is wearing a simple white shirt, black pants, and sandals. An ease of being radiates from him, and my shoulders release even more with another wave of relief.

This stranger is my driver and my first point of connection. As he guides me to the car, he assures me that everything will be okay. Continuing to smile, he confirms that he knows where we are going.

He adds, "Should be an easy drive. Not a lot of traffic this time of night."

A smile mirrors on my face as I am reminded of the goodness of humanity.

After a few silent minutes, he politely asks, "What are you seeking?"

My attention has been focused on the lights flashing through the window as we navigate the narrow streets, and I barely hear his question.

"Sorry, what was that?"

"What are you seeking? Why are you here?"

"I'm just here to visit."

He is not satisfied, and continues, "No, why are you here? Many people come here seeking something. Something spiritual. Something from God. Some sort of change. And it's true. Many people find it. They find it all over. Just look. This land is full of magic; this land is full of God."

He taps the dash of his car proudly displaying an altar with a cross, mala beads, offerings, and incense, and adds, "God is everywhere."

"You're right, I guess I am seeking something. I just don't know what it is."

He smiles wisely, "Ah, no worries. You will find it and then you will know."

He laughs and turns on the radio. Soft, lyrical music that sounds like a mixture of a harp and guitar fills the cab.

"The drive will be about an hour. We will be there soon."

Continuing to look out the window at the scenes passing by, unexpectedly, I fall asleep. The sound of his friendly voice wakes me as I peel open my eyes and orient to my surroundings.

"We are here."

In between waking and sleeping, I fumble around to grab my things and settle the fare. The driver takes my backpack out of the trunk and sets it next to the dimly lit path.

"There it is," he says.

I take a deep breath. He senses my hesitation.

Looking at me directly in the eyes, he says, "It is right down there. You will find what you do not know you are looking for."

Turning around, laughing with the wisdom of a thousand sages, he gets in the taxi and drives away. Gripping tightly onto the top strap of my backpack, I continue to hesitate. Slowly, my feet take the first steps as I summon the courage to follow the song of my heart. My thoughts flow as my body cautiously moves forward.

Dialogue and connection elevate human relationships and internal relationships. All experiences, all beings, all moments of shared energy are guideposts along the path of being. Undeniable truths exist. We must seek to find, whether consciously or unconsciously.

In each moment, we have all things and nothing. All things and nothing coexist because of each other – opposites on the wheel of creation. The ultimate potential of existence is here in the exact moment of now. Intersecting timelines of conscious beings experiencing this realm of reality weave together to create the scenes of reality.

Divine current flows through all beings, all things, and animates all living matter. We seek connection to this flow. Human moments are all held in the heart of the cosmos, the heart of God. All knowing. Not knowing. All Being. Not Being. All and nothing. The conversation between various forms is the birthplace of evolution.

As I shift to a more intentional stride, this path leads me to the most beautiful resort – thatched roofs, wooden doors, outdoor showers, a pool, and a yoga deck overlooking rice fields. My mentor is there to greet me, with a kind heart and smile.

After giving me a hug she says, "I am so glad you are here. I wanted to be sure you arrived safely. And now, I am going to bed."

Bidding her goodnight, I finish checking in. One of the staff members guides me down another dimly lit path. She shows me my room, adorned with soft white fabric, gentle lamp lighting, and dark wood furnishings. Pink petals spread on the expanse of white linen make the bed look so comfortable that I imagine sleeping for days.

She asks if I need anything.

"No, and thank you so much."

She bows and says goodnight.

Alone again, I take a few moments to settle in. Eventually, my body falls upon the immensely comfortable bed and transitions into a deep sleep.

Traveling the world – a pursuit of wanderlust – is a way to embody the archetype of the seeker. It is a privilege to experience these paramount moments of being; to see and feel the energy of different parts of this world; to touch and immerse in the waters; to lie on the sands, stones, mountains and fields; to share breath and energy with many cultures and ecosystems; and to pray and call in Divine connection at points on the Earth grid that hold ancient and future significance.

Global awareness is essential to evolution. Many believe humanity is something to be subdivided, categorized, and placed into boxes. We learn our worth based on various systems, which lead us to believe that treasures lie outside of the self or are reserved only for others. This tactic of separation keeps us distant from our shared reality.

Global awareness guides us to realize that we are more similar than we are different. A realization that is vital to activating the true essence of humanity. Even if we initially see differences, when we bring to light our shared history and our shared future, we remember that we are all so very much the same. This illumination unveils that we are each necessary and that humanity interweaves with the vast cosmic fabric.

The sun barely touches the tops of the trees when I open my eyes the next morning. Busyness in the kitchen sings sweetly through the halls and is accompanied by the most amazing smells: coconut pancakes, tea, coffee, fresh squeezed juice, and something savory. The sounds of fruit being cut join a language I cannot understand. The mixture of tones flows with an iridescence of appreciation – full of light and life.

Lured out of bed by the melody, I pull on flowing white pants and a simple top and practically float up the stairs to the yoga deck. Arriving above the sounds, things feel more subtle. Quieter notes ask for intentional listening. The song of the wind in the rice field, a soothing trickle of water, and distant conversation from locals walking along the paths, whisper a reminder to hold reverence for this space and practice.

Gathering a mat and meditation cushion, I glance around to find the perfect spot. The rising sun casts light on the dark mahogany floor, which matches perfectly with the dynamic jungle green and the softer hue of the fields that create the backdrop. Sitting in the sunbeam, I release a deep breath and then another. The feeling is idyllic. Barely a moment passes before I land in pristine reflection and contemplation.

This planet, this reality, this realm of humanity is what we all call home – a home we all share. Humans arrive to this planet to fulfill our purpose as individual souls. Our souls are multidimensional, move easily between the realms, and traverse the layers and levels of consciousness. Consciousness is in all things and beings. It is shared and individual. The mind shifts and moves with thoughts, emotions, memories, and hopes for the future. The heart is always present in a space between the realms. Our human bodies, however, exist here in this dimension of time and space.

Opening to our shared flow of being – the one spoken about by the sages and prophets – guides us through collective evolution. Exploring parts of ourselves where our resonance finds a match in another, in an experience, or in our internal landscape, ignites soul curiosity. Diving into the mysteries and the myths, and imagining the original space of creation, illuminates the wisdom necessary to manifest our potential.

To arrive intact to the next epoch, humanity must continue

seeking, learning, and going into the caves until we uncover the core truths. For eons, the ancient masters taught belief in the unbelievable. Many stories recount moments when humans performed what we call miracles, magic, or even embodied levels of superpowers. New moments are coming when we will again surprise ourselves with our capabilities. Journeying together on the path supports our highest timeline – to remember who we are. Miracles are real if we believe. We are so powerful.

Whoosh, I am back in my body. The light of the sun begins piercing my eyes from behind my eyelids. This download of wisdom feels potent, and honestly, a bit overwhelming. Blinking my eyes open, I intentionally store the wisdom in my mind and bookmark it to contemplate later.

In the now moment, my shoulders and spine start to move. My neck is tight from travel and the movement feels delicious as I slip into another experience beyond time. Moving, breathing, being in my body, and with the energy surrounding my body is soothing; inhale, exhale, expand, extend, contract, curve, flow, and breathe.

Voices coming up the stairs bring me back to the here and now. Consumed by hugs from my friends and fellow seekers, I again lock eyes with my mentor. She smiles with a knowing and an earnest desire for all of us to embody the wisdom she has been cultivating for lifetimes. The best teachers teach through actions and ways of being, and she is one of the best.

Luxurious days of movement, meditation, study, reflection, and contemplation feel essential to the evolution of my whole being.

My mentor reminds us over and over, "Feel into the full spectrum of being."

Minutes, hours, and days merge into undulating rhythms anchored by my writing practice and poring over various spiritual texts. My mind and body are immersed. Inspiration flows with the realization of the similarities found in the religious and philosophical teachings from across the world. My heart remembers all that it can while pondering the truth that humanity is more similar than we are different.

Curiosity rises around the confines of categorization, separation, why we feel the need to always be right, and the global historical narratives of imposing new beliefs on others when they differ from our own. I wonder, can humans expand our ability to receive each other with kindness and move through this life and all our lived experiences guided by familiarity?

A daily devotional prayer lands in my heart: *I pray that one day, we will all appreciate each human being as kin rather than foe.*

As the retreat ends, we are each transformed in our own ways. Leaving the group with embraces and blessings, I travel home alone.

The scenes out the window are different now as my plane lands in Doha, the capital city of Qatar. What I see is like a dream. As we move from sky to ground, I watch the cerulean mix with the light and dark tans of the sands whipped by the air – movement and hues that I have never seen. The overlap of texture and color create deep indigo and various shades of jade – a physical representation of the power of the land as it merges with the power of the wind.

This mixture reminds me of the pinnacle chapter of my favorite book – when the protagonist talks to the wind; when he remembers that his journey has always been taking him back home; when he surrenders who he was to fully embrace who he is becoming. The narrative feels achingly similar to where I find myself in this exact moment.

"Getting back home," I wistfully think, "… is now my focus."

Wheels down. We hit the tarmac with a thud and fast break. Babies start to cry as we feel the force on our bodies. Disembarking, we board buses, which take us from plane to airport. My fellow travelers are an eclectic group: families, businesspeople, young seekers, distant gazes, assorted styles of dress, diverse cultures, and different languages all crammed together.

As the stuffy, crowded transit vehicle sways back and forth, everyone appears bothered by the dry heat of desert air. Many wave hands and fans, wipe brows, and soothe small children. Admittedly, I am a bit uncomfortable. To quell my rising uneasiness, I pop in my headphones to balance my energy as I balance my oscillating body.

The bus careens along the asphalt laid in the middle of the sands and takes us toward a giant building rising at the center of the runways and connection roads. Waves of heat dance off the surface of the roads in swirls indicating the hot temperature. Sweat beads on my neck dampen the collar of my yellow linen shirt as I continue looking around at each face, each pair of eyes.

Seeking human connection, I lock eyes with someone. He is beautifully tall with light-brown curls and seems to be alone as well. Holding each other's gaze feels like a soulful knowing. Enjoying the improbable moment of overlapping narratives, we share a childish grin. The bus continues to jolt, making each of us bump into other people. We smile again – as if we are both in on some hilarious joke about the truth of this world, the playful frivolity of existence.

This traveler's eyes are blue and kind. They remind me of eyes from back home. A new yearning starts to rise. A desire for the next phase, the next chapter, the next iteration of self. If I get honest, and go even further into this feeling, I realize I am missing him. Where weeks ago something greater guided my seeking, the song of my heart, now I hear another song that is just as alluring.

As the sliding doors open, my fellow traveler and I go separate ways and never speak. We shared the briefest of moments and a sacred smile. Our silent communication imparted an essential particle of wisdom about our human condition.

Under our skin, we are all the same. We each have the systems of the body keeping us alive and in these forms. Beyond the body, we are our soul. Our souls find revelation through lived experiences and the shared consciousness of the higher dimensions. Each soul – and by extension each person – is a fractal (or repeated similar design) of the Divine, of God.

Humans are always and forever evolving. Beyond our individual experiences, we share the collective experience of being alive on this planet. Beyond the preferences, the identities, the countries, we are all human. We sing the songs of our hearts together in the places beyond the senses – our dreams, our imaginings, our prayers, our meditations, and our hopes for a happier, healthier planet. These are the realms where we reunite with the Divine flow and remember what it means to belong.

Embedded in our shared consciousness, resonating in the strings stroked to create the primal vibrations, there is an innate connection to the spark of being. The rhythms of evolution, the waves of transformation, and the beats of integration, are the changing tones that guide us back to that which we seek.

One of the core truths is that we are all connected, no matter how defiantly we try to delineate our differences. On some level, all of us seek connection, familiarity, and belonging, through relationship with self, others, this planet, and to God.

In recognizing our shared ways of being, it is essential to start in the sweet nectar of the individual. Like a rosebud unfolding, one petal at a time, each heart comes alive to its calling, becoming an elevated point on the grid of comprehension. Our waking beings coalesce on the journey of our collective evolution, just as the clouds and sand merge in the sky.

Upon entering the airport, the mélange of travelers divides into our country of origin as assigned on our passport. Casual conversations are now in a language I understand. The input of familiar tones in such a foreign place seems odd. We move through the checkpoints and ride the escalators up and into the extravagant airport.

At the top, everyone again goes their separate ways, and I stand alone surrounded by people everywhere: buzzing, talking, walking, shopping, waiting. It is a melting pot moment in the middle of the desert, steeping in the vast, beautiful sea of humanity, the similarities and the immense differences. When we look into the eyes of another, we can see our own eyes staring back. We are all connected.

Breathing deeply, I imagine the places where each person has been and the places where each person is going.

As I walk slowly, with more than enough time to get to where I am going, each step brings me more into the embodiment of who I am becoming. Walking toward the future self I know is unfolding; walking away, with appreciation, from the past self who has been brave and courageous; and walking with the present self who embodies oceans', islands', and deserts' worth of wisdom that have existed within her all along, I feel inspired.

My ego and stomach pop into my thoughts, "We are so hungry and thirsty. We must eat, now!"

The corner of my lips turn up with a smile and a laugh. The back and forth between my soul and my human is an amusing, ongoing dialogue between the realms. Following the direct instructions, I find a café, order some food, and settle in for hours in the space between. Even if just for a moment in this sea of beings – between here and there – I feel like I have found part of what I am seeking: *connection to humanity, to soul, to something within me and greater than me simultaneously.*

My own voice whispers aloud, to everyone, to no one, to my own body, heart, and soul, "We are in this together; everyone who ever has been, everyone who is, and everyone who ever will be are essential to the evolution of humanity."

# each set of eyes

we are particles vibrating
amid the impression
of permanence

but nothing is solid
that is the real truth
we are living on the skin of the apple of our planet

our individual souls arriving
shared spirit illuminating
everything in a constant state of movement

indicators point to the reality
that we really should not be here thriving the way we do
that is where the mystery lies

we constantly create suffering in ourselves and others
yet we are living in a time when compassion is rising
a demanding force to remember

returning us to the pulsation of life
that connects every living thing
our souls constantly tell us to wake up

see the light of each set of eyes
strip back the packaging of our skin
and these bodies are the same

# 5

# SUM OF ALL PARTS
## Creation & Divine Design

---

*"The ache in our heart to remember who we are*
*is the catalyst to contemplate*
*and feel the song of creation."*
*– Intuitive Wisdom*

The bus moves along the streets of Washington, D.C., as I gaze into the evening masses. Faces pass on the street. Hardly a person looks up; each is in their own head, one foot in front of the other. The pace makes it seem like everyone is going somewhere and doing something.

The air is damp from a bout of hard rain that came through not too long ago. A cup of tea is warm in my hand as an eagerness to be home wraps around my being. The darkening sky emulates my internal energy. There is softness in the transition from day to night. The sweet last drips of light weave their way between the buildings, with hints of orange, crimson, and soft rose, striped by sapphire and violet.

Spring light, spring night; gentle breezes promise something new and fresh.

My phone draws my attention as it buzzes with a message from him. Most of them are from him these days; missives, musings, poems, invitations to a shared way of being – words that create a safe space free from expectation, free from judgement. Mirroring and matching each other in creativity, curiosity, and wisdom, we explore this new phase of our relationship.

Memories of the night from last summer, when I wore the yellow dress, roar through my mind. He was visiting D.C. for the opening of an exhibit at the gallery I co-curate. An honest part of me was curious about seeing him, being close to him, and feeling our shared energy.

Knowing he would be there waiting, I raced home from work on my bike. And there he was standing in my living room clad in chambray and denim. A hint of a red bandanna peeked out of his back pocket. As he turned around, our eyes connected, my breath caught, and a pounding in my chest started to echo through my whole body.

The evening was full of laughing over whiskey, eye contact, and coy smiles. After years of pretending not to notice, we stopped resisting the feeling of connection and lost ourselves in each other. He stood in the doorway of my room as my chin lifted in a gesture to come in – an invitation. And yet, immediately we retreated. The future timeline flashed before our hearts, and we got scared. A spark in the tether between us ignited, but it was not the right time.

The next morning, I looked at his face sleeping on my pillow and thought: "He is my forever."

My flowing memories transition to a more recent moment of our shared past. A reverie within a reverie lands me in a wintry evening in Boston, just months after that potent summer night.

Coincidentally, or maybe fatefully, he was back in town from Vermont the weekend I was visiting my sister and brother-in-law. Another message sent; another invitation accepted. He met me in his 1993 Jeep Wrangler. Suave energy and the confidence of a heart full of adventure, longing, and a truer sense of self mixed with the same smile and bright cobalt eyes.

We spent the evening dancing, sharing in ecstatic expression and freedom of movement. When we arrived back to my sister's apartment, it was late. He could have said goodnight at the door. Instead, he walked me up. He could have left. He could have allowed the night to end, but he did not. We drank tea and shared our dreams.

Then the moment came: he told me he was moving west, toward mountains, coasts, and tides. My stomach turned, and I felt a panic in my heart.

"But you will be so far away."

He said, "I need to go. We're just friends. We will stay in touch."

A few weeks later, he was setting up his apartment in Seattle, and I was buying my ticket to Bali.

When I returned from my trip, the mailman handed me a post-card of the Olympic Mountains: "Thinking of you."

Then there was silence, no communication for weeks. The distance, the time difference, and the diverging paths felt so definitive. Thinking about those nights, talking about those moments, felt confusing. We were not ready.

Now, here we are at the end of spring, almost summer again, thousands of miles apart, and yet things have pivoted. Timelines feel like they are finally aligning.

Shaking my head, I bring my attention back to the present scenes of city life. The weekly chess game happens outside the shoe-repair shop as the sun continues to set. Ten or so spectators huddle around one table, with earnest looks on their faces.

Three buses have caught up to each other, making the route slow. Being on the third vehicle of the chain means my bus is relatively empty – only three riders, including myself. The woman next to me wears an Ethiopian dress. A man in a yellow jumpsuit sits with his pushcart in the front. The quiet and calm is pleasant as the bus continues navigating the city streets.

My thoughts drift again, going even further back. Layers upon layers of memories, to the soulful moment of recognition we experienced on the stairs of our college dormitory.

A young version of myself over-enthusiastically said, "Hey!"

With care and kindness, he smiled back with a gentle, "Hi."

A wave of soul-knowing rushed through my being. As if we had been together for lifetimes, when in fact it was the first time our eyes met. Unaware and very aware of the contracts we created before we were born, in the realms beyond, our souls knew each other.

Since that meeting on the stairs, our timelines overlapped and intertwined – casual friends, to trusted confidants, to roommates, to long-distance dear friends. Through the years, other people held our hearts and our hands. Now, our hearts and our hands reach toward each other. All the parts of our story are coming together.

Waking, dreaming, remembering what has been, and imagining what will be, my thoughts are only of him. The ever-encroaching timeline where we are finally together and free to be everything we create in our missives and musings crystallizes. Lured by the tingle of connection that activated when his eyes met mine so many years ago, I know our paths finally align. How exactly is another question entirely.

A soft smile graces my lips as I envision him. In my imagination, he is dressed in dark wool and a collared shirt that matches the color of his eyes. Sipping slowly on a cup of black coffee and gazing out at the Olympic Mountains, I imagine him typing me a message with the slightest of smiles on his face. Two hopeless romantics start to feel a glimmer of hope.

Easing into another flowing reverie, my thoughts shift as I lean my head against the cool glass of the window and close my eyes.

Together, we are learning to co-create our reality. We share words and energy. We send thoughts and longing between the miles. The creative life force in all of us has a way of making itself known. Writers organize words. Makers make objects. Storytellers guide us through emotions we often cannot access on our own. We all create in some way. Our interpretation, the movement of our thoughts, becomes form in the world. Each mark or knot is a reordering of material. Processes happen and then something exists. That is the way. The why is more complicated.

Where some people find connection and questions are seemingly answered, others become lost in the explanation. Many more creatives wait for someone to give them permission, unable to find the courage to claim what is theirs.

Too often, humans stay caught in the "what if" or "if only." We forget that we are all conduits of knowing. Divine wisdom flows through every aspect of our being. Our innate creative life force always sways and dances to the internal song.

Each of us can activate the creator within and choose to create the life we desire. This activation allows for the experience of creation to become embodied. We need both mind and body. When in alignment, we find the courage to do, write, say, and build what makes us feel most alive. This quality of aliveness, living on the edge of the contemplation of curiosity and the action of creation, makes us undeniably human.

Another wave of warm breeze mixed with city fumes wafts through the space as the doors on my bus open at NW 14th and Columbia. My eyes open to watch the man with his pushcart navigate down the aisle to the exit at the back. Slowly lowering his cart down each step, he moves with intention. Curiosity guides my thoughts: Has this man lived his whole life in this neighborhood? If we cross paths again, will we notice?

Others join the evening commute. Most are looking down at their phones, while some are staring into the distance. One group of riders is full of laughter and vitality. The enthusiasm of this new company creates background noise to the track playing in my headphones – a song he sent to me with the note, "This makes me think of you."

Two more blocks and it will be my turn to exit the scene. After I pull the cord for a stop, the bus slows and the doors open.

"Thank you, driver," I call from the back of the bus.

Grabbing the top strap of my backpack, my steps feel easy as I head out into the evening.

Humans strive to do this – the making of our lives. From simple moments of choosing the clothes we wear each day, to selecting tile for the kitchen counter, to more complicated endeavors of who to love, how to love, when to stay and when to go, we build our lives. We create details and nuance, like brush strokes on a canvas. We fill our homes, plant our gardens, and choose ways of life. We do all of this while we form the more obscure, the less tangible, the creation of thought and intelligence. Strings of being come together, allowing us to birth into the manifested world the scenes from our imagination.

Everything starts in our imaginings. Conception happens in the mind. The wish, the want, the idea, the spark of energy, and the fundamental inspiration focus our attention and intention on the process of bringing something from the mystical realm into the material, three-dimensional world. Everything in all the universes, within universes, starts with the formation of a thought. From the mind of God to the mind of humans, and every dimension in between, what we believe, we eventually see.

A creation is simply the sum of all parts. Slowing down, identifying the parts, and learning how they go together is how we comprehend our vast and complex reality. From this comprehension, we access our capacity to make worlds within worlds.

World-making, life-forming, reality-building – all require an innate desire for creation. Desire is the motivating force of aligned action. This aspect of all beings comes from the energy of the soul and the accumulated memories of all experiences of all lifetimes. Rather than processing our lives as isolated, choosing to comprehend how they relate to the greater journey of the soul contextualizes individual desires throughout the course of each lifetime in relationship to the desire of the soul.

Soul desire drives each of us to experience the life necessary for individual evolution. Desire gets us out of our own way so that we can do the things that scare us, to say the things we are nervous to speak aloud, to send the love note, or make the call. Being human is a cycle of desire and creation, both infinite and finite.

When I am home in the comfort of my bed, flowing tides of thoughts and dreams welcome me into sleep.

His handsome face – with his distinct features, scar on his forehead, and golden blonde hair – comes in and out of focus through the wanderings of my mind. We are on an expanse of beach bathed by the light of the sunset as a line of suitors walks away. He is the last man standing; he picks me up and spins me, just like he did in Paris during our semester abroad. This scene, this dream, feels so real. A sound in the distance draws my attention. My alarm is going off – it is already morning.

As the sun rises over the city, I decide to go for a walk. Dressing in light denim pants, an oversized cardigan, and my favorite sandals, I grab my bag and quietly head out the front door of the townhouse. Hints of spring decorate the warm morning. The colors, the smells, the hopeful way of being emerge from every petal, leaf, and ray of sunshine. Pink cherry blossoms are in full bloom on the branches. Slowing down allows me to feel the details so often missed when I am rushing from one place to the next or traveling the musings of my mind. Immersing myself in the sensory experience, I stroll slowly in the quiet, calm of the morning.

Pausing at the intersection, I notice a spider web, then a drop of water on a leaf. The image shows my inverted reflection – it feels fitting. Everything is shifting and realigning. Above and below meet each other as primary opposites, knowingly creating the inverse of the other to expand the awareness of the pair. Universes encased in elemental power are formed by oppositional relationships.

Life is not linear. The future guides the present, which tells the story of the past. All are necessary to make sense of the other. The buds on the rosebush remind me of Divine design. They open because of an attunement to the greater rhythms of this reality. The unfolding happens one petal at a time in the cycle of being.

A car honks and I look up. The "real" world moves by – rushing, wasting, wanting. Another wave of freshness in the air grabs my attention. Closing my eyes, I synchronize with the energy that surrounds me and is within me. It is not human – it is something entirely different, and yet it is coexisting in the same space. A combination of inputs and ephemeral information weave together from multiple dimensions to create this exact moment, right here, right now. Fully alive, hand to heart, I return to center.

The notion of center, the idea of the middle or median, represents the concept of returning to the mid-line. A physical location of the body found in the spine and a persistent energy existing within and beyond the body. The center is where all the parts come together; it is the nexus of life force and purpose.

This nexus is the core essence that holds me, holds all of us, together. Magnetic, electric. Frequency and vibration. Attracting me to others, attracting me to myself. Constantly and consistently turned on by the pulse, the rhythm, the spiral of creation. The place of our energetic center – a core of light and intelligence – is where everything makes sense.

As I continue to walk the city streets, my thoughts lure me away from the details of the now moment and back into the labyrinth of contemplation. From one end of a spectrum to the other, never staying too long in any one locality, I explore my intuition as it guides me through the kaleidoscope of being.

A realization lands. He brings me back to center – my tether to this earth, to being human. His grounding and consistent dependability mirrors what I strive to feel internally. It matches my desire to find the mid-line, the calm balance – where harmony and peace flood my body and soul. As I long for a feeling of union with the spacious evolution along my central channel and with someone in the external world who embodies the same level of curiosity about this magical existence, his energy pulls me toward him now more than ever before.

Stopping at a park bench, I sit. Closing my eyes in reflection, my imagination again takes me to him, the feeling of him. In my mind, I see the light that dances in the blue of his eyes. I imagine being wrapped in the warmth of his kindness. Inspired by his curated rugged wardrobe and chosen aesthetic details – from rolled denim to dinners by candlelight – a curious smile graces my lips as I think about the words he writes in the tiny notebook kept safe in the front pocket of his waxed jacket. Maybe one day I will know what questions truly dance between his thoughts and his heart. Blissful attraction activates between the miles.

My thoughts shift as they carry me to the energy of my loved ones, and I reflect on their details of being – my family, my friends and all their shared nuances of character and displays of uniqueness. A soft energy of endearment rises in my chest. Imagining a stranger, I see their humanness in their eyes. Imagining every human on this planet, I reflect on our kindred ways.

Each person is breathing and being – we all share this breath. The same breath has supported humanity for millennia. The many beings that came before us and the many beings that will come after us all breathe the same air.

Feeling deeper into the truth of our shared breath, I know now that this planet herself is breathing. We will all at some point take our last breath in a body, and yet the planet will keep breathing, pulsing, and spiraling through the cosmos. When I fully give myself to this core truth, I am in my center of knowing – completely alive and driven by a soul desire – to call in the energy of love rather than trapping myself in the energy of fear. A liberation of my own creation.

We are, as are all details of our lives, essential aspects of the Divine design. Each undulation of our human vessel is mirrored and matched in the great vastness of the cosmos. Each breath, each petal, each memory, each hope, each lived experience creates the landscape of existence. Spiraling, cycling, and returning to center, eternally and forever. From the song of the heart to blossoms on the branch, from stage to street, from canvas to simple love notes, an exquisiteness exists in the reflections and forces that combine to make reality.

My eyes, as always, look up to the light of our sun. The warmth is delicious as it pairs with the scent of the light pink roses that delineate the paths of the park. Pausing to receive this wisdom on this bench in the capital city is so similar to the way I felt in Paris last year. I indulge in the details of here and now. Vast shades of pink and yellow dance. Joining the roses are rhododendrons, azaleas, tulips, and daffodils, accompanied by the purple hues of lilacs starting to open toward the sky.

These details, this Divine design in which we all exist, has always been and will always be what is molding us and our reality. It inspires us with each breath to hear the song of creation.

My phone buzzes in my bag; I wonder what he has written to me today.

what are we

a curious thing the cycles of life
the complexity seemingly simple
birth and ultimate death

the unknowns and knowns
the whos, the whats
the hers, hims, they, them

but what is known?
something that is past
for if it is not past, then has it ever really been?

when is anything in full being?
what could have been?
that is the only real unknown

for it never was
and never will be
a simple creation of the mind

the dreamer dreams
the thinker thinks
the lover loves

what are we if not products trapped by our signifiers
identities encased in projections
of what we are becoming?

are we tangible?
we touch and feel
we are entangled

but why? and how?
can we release the categorization
and expand beyond the confines?

if we could know in some way how everything will be
would the world continue to offer
the crisp truth of the eternal now?

or
is the not knowing
the feeling of being alive?

the feeling of being alone searching
the wanting and waiting for something, someone
the innate desire of being seen and felt by another

I said, "This reminds me of times past. Isn't everything passed time?"
the memory of a previous moment dictating the reality of the future
revolving around the possibility of the present

everything looping in on itself
only to find the beginning and end infinitely connected
tides roll in and out

there are simple truths
constantly changing
constantly constant

# 6

# COMINGS AND GOINGS
## Choice & Change

---

*"Existing as an emanation of the Divine,*
*we are responsible for our actions and reactions.*
*Choice is the sovereign right of each individual."*
*– Intuitive Wisdom*

Thick clouds hover over the skyline as I peer through the dirty kitchen window toward the neighbor's deck. At this hour, the energy of the city feels still, and cars drive by our townhouse only every so often. I watch the world while I wait – for my coffee to drip, for my life to change, for our decision to feel real.

A gentle breeze greets me as I open the window. While it is still unseasonably warm, fall hints at its arrival with a whisper on the wind and a golden glow on the branches.

As if peeking in to say, "I'm coming. It is time to let everything go."

The anticipation that everything in my life, not only the seasons, is shifting into a new phase of being makes sleep elusive. These early mornings are sacred, and I savor every moment as I know my days in this townhouse, this city, this chapter of my life are ending.

Quietly moving back down the stairs to my room, trying not to wake my roommates, I slip into my safe nest away from it all. As I sip slowly from the steaming cup, I wrap a scarf over my shoulders for comfort – even though the air is warm. Moments later, sunlight pierces the clouds and pours in through the basement window. Tangerine swirls mix with hues of rose and lavender, creating a dreamlike palette as pre-dawn rays blaze over the capital.

As I rock slowly in my chestnut-brown rocking chair, an inspiration invites me over to my drawing desk. Slow movements guide me as I follow the creative call.

The sound of the neighbor's gate opening and closing momentarily catches my attention. Someone else is up and out before the sun has fully risen. The drumbeat of action motivates the people of this city – forward momentum and marching toward progress and the future.

When I moved here for graduate school, just weeks after returning from Vietnam and Laos, this steady pulse was enticing. My art career started to thrive, and so much was on the horizon – a new chapter welcoming new ways of being.

During my second semester, in pursuit of deepening my spiritual practices, I registered for an elective course in yoga and meditation. This independent thread became a beloved job, community, and chrysalis of transformation. Since the moment I arrived at this vibrant metropolis, abundance has graced me with like-minded friends, extravagant experience, and overwhelming opportunity.

Sitting at my drawing desk, pen in hand, I reflect on all that has transpired over the last four years. The pen now moves as I make marks on the page. Swirling lines of varying gradation, weight, and length, create something new, and yet similar to my style of work. The meditative motion eases my mind and drifts me into a hypnotic calm. Movements of the pen mirror the movements of the clouds. The process of creation absorbs my full attention, slowly leading to another portal of reverie.

Choice and chance are guideposts along the path. Free will – the smallest choices and those that feel paramount – is where the human defines the path of soul evolution. Choice is the right of each individual soul incarnate in a body. Moments of choices loop into and through a series of chances or predetermined events.

Chance lives in the dimension of the unknown, the "what ifs." The current of chance can make us uncomfortable, unsure, and uncertain. These ripples often lead us into fear if we allow our energy to flow without awareness. Chance is the swirling patterns of seeming chaos. With awareness, the highest expression of chance embraces trust in the choices of the soul.

Choice and chance weave together to form a network of experience during each lifetime and guide us to live the necessary timelines and narratives for our soul-led evolution. Together, they create the beauty of the now moment.

Pausing to look at my work, I pull a fresh page from my painting pad. Shifting to the creation of color and form, I instinctively add pours of colored ink onto the page. Pigments interface on the surface, forming organic, asymmetrical shapes. Lifting the page, I hold the paper just long enough for the ink to drip in various directions. Unplanned marks form the most fascinating moments of the painting.

Gathering my brushes, dipping them into midnight blue, cadmium yellow, and red, the primaries mix in magnificent hues to add precise details to the composition. My steady hand navigates the paper with curiosity of what will come from this practice of intuitive creation.

Thoughts continue as patterns merge and emerge in unison to formulate an image.

When we choose to change, the trajectory of life reveals itself anew. We go from simply surviving to living with awareness and eventually thriving. We determine if a situation is causing harm or if a situation is nourishing and nurturing. We evaluate if we are safe, happy, healthy, and loved. Depending on the observation, we get to choose our response. Prioritizing that which is primary for our stability and foundation supports our trust in self and soul wisdom (the perspective of multiple lifetimes).

Stagnation is doing things the same way over and over. If we want to change something, then we must choose to make the change. Hope for the future requires the bravery necessary to walk a new path. Blazing our own trail means choosing to do things differently. While potentially uncomfortable, intentionally interfacing with moments of choice guides us to decide how to be and how to receive.

Just as naturally as it started, my drawing and painting session ends. The brush, the creative flow, and the thoughts in my mind all quiet as I lean back in my chair. Releasing a long exhale while scanning the room, my attention catches on the little piles of things covering the surfaces. Bills, old studio notes, and invitations to the events of the season provide a physical representation of my abundant life.

This life – this creative, wanderlust life – the one I dreamed of for so long, is my reality. And yet, I am choosing to leave. Wants and desires conceived by an older version of self no longer resonate with this emerging version of self. Now, every detail feels like an artifact of a different timeline and a dissolving identity.

Pushing a pile into the trash, I transition from my desk to my meditation cushion. Craving the balance of creative pursuit and spiritual awakening, I satiate my desire with twenty minutes of stillness and breath. My timer dings and I continue my practice by moving my body through a simple routine of yoga postures. Pausing my body as light continues to pour through the window, I jot a few notes in my journal.

The words read: "In the midst of currents of change, we get to choose how to react, how to live, and how to move through this world. We each get to choose."

As I lie down on my yoga mat in exhilaration, many emotions flood my being.

Part of me cannot believe this is happening – a new city, new life, new way of being. Part of me is more than ready. The part in disbelief couples with a hint of hesitation. There is so much, and so many, that I am leaving behind. Excitement and sadness interlace hands in the paradox of shifting timelines.

It happened fast, this choice point. Just weeks ago, when he joined me on a yoga retreat in Nicaragua, we knew it was time. Standing in vulnerability, I told him I loved him. His entire being released into an embodiment of ease. He was not ready to say it back, although the validation of hearing these words allowed him to feel the truth. Our alignment had finally arrived.

Staring at my ceiling, I flow into a practice of inquiry.

"Does it make sense? I am letting go of everything I have worked so hard for …"

My heart affirms: "Yes! It is time."

Expectations and limitations persuade us to make certain choices. Many of us think or have been taught that we need to do so much to prove ourselves. We think there is some grand finish line. Marching to the beat, onward and upward, often we choose things not because we want to, but because we feel like we should, trying to stave off disappointment or regret. We obsess over every detail and lose ourselves in the anxiety that we might do something wrong. Unconscious patterns of being start looping until we find the courage to change them. Empowerment comes when we remember that we get to choose what to do with this life.

"Am I just letting it all go?" I question aloud. "Or is this all a part of the greater plan?"

My heart pours answers through my thoughts.

While we cannot control all circumstances, and many experiences arrive due to convergence with other timelines, we can choose how we interact with each choice point. Guided by free will, desire, and the memory of all lifetimes, we can align our actions and reactions with our soul wisdom. Choices made in alignment with the journey of the soul are choices that hold the higher expression of experience.

In the context of the multiverse, we are here on Earth because we chose to be here. Connection to the power of choice guides us to take aligned action and, when necessary, shift the trajectory of our narratives and timelines. In these shifts, evolution is apparent. The energy created during the process of evolution – small or large – broadcasts through our shared consciousness to other aspects of soul. This process upgrades the collective wisdom of our multidimensional beings.

Elevating the relationship between human free will and soul wisdom can last infinite incarnations. Innumerable choice points arrive in a lifetime. Elevation of choice and aligned action is a cyclical relationship and an essential aspect of evolving our shared consciousness.

Looking at the time, I realize that – in this dimension – I need to get dressed and out of the house. Rushing to gather my items for the day, throwing on comfortable yoga clothes, brushing my teeth, and placing my empty mug in the sink in the kitchen, I swing my bike around from the back room and head out the door. Each moment is a choice of what to do and how.

Leaves crunch as my tires roll through the iron gate. With my backpack slung on my back, I ride under the rich aquamarine blue that now paints the sky. The early morning clouds dissolve into mist. As always, my thoughts continue.

It is a privilege to live a life where we get to make choices, upgrade our ways of being, and evolve. Choice is powerful: to choose to stay or go at any moment; to choose to change a behavior or keep doing it the way we always have; to choose to listen to our hearts, or not; and to choose to activate our intuition and connection to soul. Even the simpler decisions like coffee or tea, sit longer or stand up, sleep in or wake up, guide our path of being.

While I hold my handle bars and pedal in steady rotations, my mind stills and breath flows. Shifting to coast downhill, listening to the clicking of my tire – the one he fixed when he was last in town – I roll to stop at a red light. My left foot grounds down on the pavement as I wait for the stoplight to change.

I hook my foot back into the toe cage on my pedal, and autumn air caresses my face. The familiarity of this position reminds me of the freedom I feel while nimbly navigating the city on two wheels – a chosen and intentional way of being, one revolution after another. My body comes more online, more alive, just like the stellar dance of all things everywhere – spiral upon spiral upon spiral of aliveness flowing through the cosmos.

Spending my day working at the yoga studio, I enjoy every moment of sharing space, energy, and laughter with friends and community. Early evening light guides me as I ride through Dupont Circle toward the Foggy Bottom neighborhood to check on my art installation. The exhibit received major accolades and acclaimed responses from various elite minds of the art scene. The installation comes down next week and is likely my last showing in the city.

A darkening sky indicates the passing of a full day. While it is late, I decide to meet a friend for dinner at our favorite Thai restaurant – a ritual of companionship and conversation.

Pedaling home, I start thinking again – always thinking. This pensive quality of being is sometimes quite exhausting. Contemplation, however, leads me toward revelations. The tone of my thoughts has shifted with the energy of the day, and tonight I land in a memory from Botswana.

Last January, I traveled to Gaborone, Botswana, for an artist residency with the Art in Embassies program. After the curator saw my MFA thesis exhibition, she offered me the commission to create a site-specific installation of three-dimensional woven fabric for the ambassador's house. Ushering in a piece of art that felt new, edgy, and fresh was an honor I gladly accepted. Eager to yet again experience adventure, culture, and creation, I felt my wanderlust rise.

The trip was pristine – touring the countryside with a personal driver, staying at a luxury hotel, presenting lectures, talking on radio shows, and sitting for a television interview. Experiencing an international platform to discuss art, culture, theory, and philosophy was a dream come true.

On the final afternoon of my residency, I sat on the patio of the Ambassador's house, drinking rooibos tea and listening to the patterns of the rain. Each afternoon for the final four days of the trip, I collaborated with a team of local artists to create the site-specific installation. They taught me the power of community and taking time for afternoon tea, while I taught them to think about color, form, and material in new ways. The afternoons were a priceless exchange of profound connection.

Together we wove the fabric to create shape, line, and shadow. Strips of yellow, green, blue, pink, and red fabric – that were once t-shirts from various members of our communities – merged and overlapped, creating geometric visuals. Intentionally placed lights cast soft, gray shadows on the white plaster walls. The spectator could walk under and through the archway formed by the fabric.

One of my fellow artists exclaimed, "Wow, now this is art!" as he interacted with the full sensory experience of the installation.

The emphatic statement was in response to the dialogue that guided the trip. The question he was answering was the question I posed during my first lecture.

It was the same question that guided my master's thesis: "What is art?"

Even now, as I ride my bike through the streets of my beloved city, a flutter of excitement moves through me as I ponder this question. This creative current has been so close to me for the past four years – weaving its way into and through my waking world and my dream world, and beating to the pulse of my curiosity and artistic pursuits.

This question was the reason I applied and decided to go to graduate school. The reason I continued to engage in the dialogue years after graduating. The reason I stayed up late, thinking, sketching, and researching. As I reflect on this memory, I notice a shift in my curiosity. "What is art?" is no longer the question singing the song of my internal yearning.

A revelation lands: *a true change in focus and recalibration of desire happen within.*

The questions now at the forefront of my heart, what my soul craves to know, to feel, and to uncover, dive deeper into our Divine human experience. What is partnership? What is home? What does it feel like to create a family? What spiritual truths are yet to be unveiled?

Warm air kisses my face. The smell of dried leaves on the ground greets my nose. An ache overcomes my being as I realize that to choose one thing, I must let go and step fearlessly toward the shifting melody of my internal chorus.

My heart softly sings the verses of truth. Reminding me to trust in soul wisdom, because our soul lovingly chooses the experiences necessary to provide moments of transformation and evolution.

As I begin to fully embrace the transition to another timeline – upgrading, evolving, dissolving, and emerging – more truths land in my field of awareness. Multiple channels of consciousness require multiple iterations of self. Letting go of one version creates space for a new reality to land. Love and loss. The ups and downs. The comings and goings. Endings that lead to beginnings. Choice and chance. Soul and human. Change is constant and so is freewill.

All these truths coalesce to nurture the fertile ground on which we birth ourselves from ourselves in creation of something new. This becoming requires the interface of choice and chance, a willingness to change, and a belief that humanity can become a version of human who is closer to the Source of all things.

Hopping off my bike and rolling through the iron gate, I pause at the brick steps of the shared townhouse. My eyes, with bated breath, search for a glimpse of the moon.

Silencing my mind, I listen for the slightest rustle of leaves in the maple tree and the rush of the city in the distance. Quieting even more, I create space to hear the innermost currents of my heart. Gaining momentum, the subtle energy collides with me, in me, knocking me off the course of hesitation just enough to clear my fear of letting go and hear the sweet resonance of now.

My eyes shift to the orchid sitting on the basement windowsill in my room. Just when least expected, a new bloom has opened. The sweetest reminder to listen for change.

Pulling my phone from my backpack and scrolling through the messages, a warmth rises in my chest. An excitement starts to brew. A new desire – a true wanting – surfaces. Something that is ancient, future, and good. An echo of a promise swirls through the timelines and ignites my heart with strands of golden light.

The poems, the long-distance flirtation, the contemporary courting, the earnest longing for each other, the memories of ten years of friendship, and the contract of souls made in the space beyond all weave together as an inspiration to follow the path toward the future, our future.

My phone dings in my hand. Another message arrives, as does a smile.

"Simple journeys: morning coffee, mountain views, evening music – now request a partner. Your hair, eyes, lips consume my thoughts. Curled up in bed, windows open. A cool fall breeze demands an extra blanket. Thoughts of you bring more warmth. Looking forward to future nights shared."

## we each belong

we begin again
with a focus not felt for some time
hearing a familiar voice from the cavern within

too often anxious thoughts shroud the heart
creating illusion
release now the casing held tightly around this most precious jewel

complementarity exists in all things
two opposites simultaneously pulsing
dependent on the other for their own manifestation

the pulsation of the breath
is itself an oppositional activation
inhale, exhale

create a homecoming
to whom we truly are
an internal community where we each belong

just like the roots of the trees
trust the heart even if not seen
receive the dynamic experience of aliveness

just like the tides
slowly crafting the cliffs
allow choice to transform the stories of lives well-lived

# 7

# LESSONS OF THE LANDSCAPE

## The Mind & Ease

---

*"The mind extends beyond the body.*
*It connects to multiple dimensions and timelines.*
*It is a fierce power when wielded with intention."*
*– Intuitive Wisdom*

Mountains are infinitely majestic – jagged peaks, dominance, stillness, and power. The Cascades, dotted with volcanic peaks, emerald lakes, and old-growth forests, hold even more mystery. As we drive, heavy snow creates a mirage of a tunnel on the other side of the windshield. With each falling flake, the precipitation accumulates, and I gaze in wonder at the landscape.

"Did you expect this much snow?" I ask.

"No," he says calmly and keeps driving.

To be honest, neither of us expected this much snow. And not just snow, but the wet, heavy snow of spring.

This morning, as the fog lifted, we drove east from Seattle toward the sunrise. The directions showed that the drive would be four hours, and we would arrive at the trailhead well before midday, affording us plenty of time to complete the five-mile hike to Snow Peak cabin before sunset. Unbeknownst to us, the mountain pass on Highway 2 had closed, due to a recent, unexpected snowslide.

We drove all the way up to the orange, fluorescent barricades just feet in front of the collapsed snowbank. Snow, rocks, and ice covered what should have been the road. Laughing at the situation, we turned around to inquire about an alternate route at the ranger's station.

"Well, you can drive back into the city, go south, and try to cross the mountains on the other pass. Or you can go even farther south and try to avoid the snow all together. Either way, you must go all the way back to the city and hope for the best."

Grinning at each other and then looking back at the ranger, in unison we said, "Thanks so much."

"Good luck with the snow."

As we stop for gas and prepare our reroute around the mountain, we realize the divergence shifts the drive to nine hours instead of four. Full of ease, we start our new route to the trailhead.

Long driving hours pair with a soundtrack of solid vocals and crescendos from our favorite artists. Just weeks into merging our lives, the cocoon of adoration holds us.

"I suppose this is not so bad," I offer.

He interlaces his fingers with mine and kisses the freckles on the back of my hand.

"I agree. This is perfect."

The extra time on the road gifts us views of the Scablands – the stunning eastern Washington landscape created by the glaciers of the ice ages. As we pass impressive geological vistas, stratified formations, and massive rock outcroppings, we see with our own eyes why this area boasts to be one of the more unique geological makeups in the continental United States.

We pull into the parking lot after dark, tired but in high spirits. Folding down the back seat of the Subaru, rolling out our camping pads and sleeping bags, we quickly fall into much needed rest. Our minds float between waking and dreaming.

Whether awake or asleep, the mind forms worlds within worlds, beliefs within beliefs, and dreams within dreams. The flowing energy of the mind creates an internal landscape with infinite summits and valleys. Traveling into the mind is awe-inspiring. From thoughts, to imagination, to dreams, the dimensions of the mind are vast, beautiful, and complex.

Our cognitive synapses strengthen by activating over and over like a muscle. Emotions and experiences fortify or dissolve in the realm of the mind. We think about a warm breeze and sunshine, and we feel lighter. We think about a house burning down, and we feel panic. We can convince ourselves of anything. What we think, we eventually become.

The journey into, with, and through the currents of the mind is not a trip for the faint-hearted. Re-charting the trodden pathways of the internal landscape requires patience and persistence. Too much, too fast throws us off-balance, falling into traps of foreign and snarling creations of our thoughts. Forming an evolved relationship with our internal world opens channels to expansive realities and dimensions, where we build new merger points between external reality and internal imagination.

Imagination is the birthplace of reality. Memories of times past and hopes of a future state are the inspiration for everything ever created. Dreams are as true as the moments when eyes are open. Our mind holds the stories and then shares it through the body, voice, written word, creative pursuits, and other forms of communication.

And though I sleep, my mind is alive.

Awoken by the light dancing through the branches of the trees, our bodies feel achy from sleeping in the car. Rising to dress in layers of winter gear to guard against the elements, we adjust our packs and begin our walk into the forest.

Within ten feet, we hear and feel a crack. The snowpack releases and our feet sink down into wet white terrain. Five miles of this is not sustainable. Returning to the car, we reassess our gear and packs, deciding what is necessary and what is not.

With only one pair of snowshoes, together we determine that he should be the one to wear them. He will chart the path up the mountain and carry the heavier pack. After I latch a pair of crampons onto my hiking boots and readjust my straps, we set off again. My feet follow his footsteps – step by step by step.

The meditative motion and acute attention on where to move and how, lulls my energy into a practice of mindfulness. Occasionally stopping to notice the details of the mountain landscape, I spend the first hour of the hike in the stillness of my mind.

As a powerful energy field, the mind flows in and around the physical body, receiving and giving data and information. The mind is not the brain or a physical part of our being. Rather, it is a limitless, immaterial aspect of our energetic being.

The mind is one of the channels of intuition. The mind is an access point to pre-cognitive knowing. The mind is the vehicle for multidimensional communication and travel in meditation and dreams. The mind is home of the ego. The mind and the heart, some would say, are one in the same. The mind weaves into and with consciousness and soul, though they are not the same.

The practice of mindfulness invites the mind to still. Paying attention to the task at hand and listening to the breath are the only objectives. Mindfulness is a way of being in the mind, rather than consumed by thoughts. A practice of noticing and simplifying, rather than listening to the ego, traveling into imagination, or inviting contemplation and reflection. Mindfulness is a practice of presence.

Feeling a surge of mind energy in my body and beyond, my practice of mindfulness ends. Switching the channel to the etheric realm of my imagination, I enter currents of thought that feel intimate and comfortable.

The lands of imagination merge our waking world awareness with the infinite possibilities of our internal world. Our imaginings validate our capacity to access reality beyond the five senses. Imagination creates portals between our physical dimension and other dimensions – an energetic bridge connecting us to our multidimensional existence. When we allow our imagination to hold space and verify the details of our internal world, we open our energy to our infinite potential. Imagination is not simply fanciful fantasy; it is, in fact, a necessary tool for creating reality.

Just like in the land of dreams, while I walk, my mind is fully alive.

The farther up and into the forest we go, the more my mind starts to swirl. The elation of yesterday starts dancing with fear. The beauty of the landscape weaves with the unknown trail. A dynamism in my thoughts arouses excitement and caution. With each angled slope between the tree lines, my adrenaline and anxiety increase.

Fearful of getting lost, falling down the mountain, triggering an avalanche, or crossing paths with a mountain lion, my mind starts to weave stories and hold focused awareness of my surroundings. My thoughts conjure the potential of mythical creatures, portals to realms beyond the senses, and alternate timelines reveal themselves as possibilities.

My legs feel heavy, and my toes are prickly with cold. My breath shortens on the incline. Frustrated and tired, I keep going. Slowly, I remember to deepen the rhythm of my inhale and exhale to strengthen my stride. He is steady. He is always steady.

Convincing my aching thighs to keep going, my feet find more confidence. Coaxing long breaths in through my nose and out through my mouth acclimates my body and lungs to the increasing elevation and thin, crisp mountain air.

Wrestling my energy from one thought to the next persuades the threatening clouds of my mind to find a gentler tone and less anxiety. This recalibration of movement, breath, and thought is holy choreography keeping me internally and externally engaged and aware. Soon, my feet, my breath, my thoughts, and the internal rhythmic tapestry known only to me become a melody.

Two hours into the hike, my nervous system shifts gears, and my energy starts to calm. Our pace settles into a quiet flow, and the snow hardens as we get closer to the tree line. Step by step. Breath by breath. Thought by thought.

The brain, the nervous system, and the other cognitive pathways of the body are the hardware system for thought. We feel our thoughts throughout the whole body, not just in the head, where we tend to identify them as located. This full-body system requires intentional, daily recalibration. Everything works in collaboration, rather than isolation.

The vastness of these connections can be studied for lifetimes. The trillions of synapses in the physical body match, mirror, and expand in the energetic field and network of the mind existing beyond the body. Countless contemporary and ancient teachings catalogue this knowledge.

Similarly, the canons of timeless wisdom teach that the mind and the ego, while we are in bodies, are inseparable companions. The ego is the part of our being that keeps us human. The ego is an aspect of our core essence and programs our identity. It is a critical part of our ancient biological processing system that encourages us to stay alive and experience this human dimension as long as possible.

Every moment, thoughts weave between the infinite mind and the limited ego. The quality of thought shifts depending on where we source the mental data. Thoughts can be controlled and manipulated when stuck in the ego – caught in fear and worry. And yet, there are many moments during each incarnation when indulging in our ego is exactly what the soul needs to experience to unfold into its potential. Sometimes we need to go into the dark to find the light. Down to up. Fall to rise.

Beauty exists in the ego if we are willing to nurture its purpose as a tool of evolution. We do not need to dissolve the ego completely. Rather, when we release from the stagnation caused by limited thinking, we cultivate a balanced relationship with our ego and belief in our potential. Thoughts are activated and liberated when expanded in the mind – flowing with trust and expression.

He pauses as I follow his footprints up the inclined trail. Looking up toward the flakes still falling from the sky, we share a moment in time, space, and each other's energy. His eyes twinkle as they reflect the light bouncing off the snow. Noticing the somewhat distant look on my face, the one I get when I am navigating my internal landscape, he gives me a knowing smile. He, too, has been deep in his thoughts. Another trait we share, appreciate, and value in the other.

No words are spoken, only silent communication. He lifts my chin and brushes a snowflake off my cheek with a gentle caress. Then, he kisses me with intention and I feel a rush of heat through my whole body. With a grin, confirming he felt it too, he hands me the canteen and encourages me to drink water before we keep going.

As he starts walking, I wait and watch him for a moment. His stride, his knowledge, and his steadfastness all radiate with wisdom. His strength reflects years of tending to his form. Every inch of his stature exudes the energy of protector. He has been and will always be the motivating force that keeps us going.

As we walk, I do my best to catch my bearings. Only two other people have been on the trail. They were going down. We are going up. It is just the two of us for miles in the vast, snow-covered wilderness. Distracted for a moment by snow falling off a branch, I catch the edge of the snowbank and stumble.

I call out to him to stop.

He calls back to ask, "Is it mental or is it physical?"

Frustration flashes as I scrunch my face in disdain. Deciding to remain silent, I wave that I am okay. The rhythm of one foot after another continues as my aching muscles carry me ever forward. My attention returns to my internal world.

A shift of expression happens when we find the path in the internal landscape that is guided by the higher frequencies of mind and soul. On this path, the veils lift or drop completely, and thoughts become portals to the eternal truths and the Divine. We remember that everything is sacred, especially the energy of the mind.

Deep in contemplation, we walk. Hours later, with short pauses for food, water, and encouragement, we crest the ridge.

He calls out, "I see it."

Catching up to him, I exclaim, "You've got to be kidding me."

Laughing and slumping my shoulders, I let out an exasperated sigh. The cabin is still quite far in the distance. Though he is right, we can see it. Another thirty minutes of plodding up and down through deep, cold snow lies ahead. We keep walking.

We finally reach the cabin and relief washes over us. Dropping our packs, we survey the accommodations, which are sparse and cozy. He immediately starts stacking kindling and logs for a fire. Something about his silent devotion to create safety and comfort brings a smile to my face.

Reflecting upon the summit and our shared accomplishment, I smile even more and say, "If you do not love me after this ..."

He grins, creating the creases alongside his eyes that appear when he is being completely genuine and says, "If you still love me after this ..."

We look at each other and laugh together. A laugh that only friends who have known each other over a decade can share. And then, we pause. As the fire catches flame in the hearth, he gets up and walks toward me. He holds my face in both hands. Looking me in the eyes – cobalt blue to hazel green – he gives me a kiss. Soft, gentle, and confident; a declaration of love and pride. An affirmation of this life that is now, this life that has been, and this life that will be. We are now so much more than friends.

The fire crackles, and we clink our glasses in what feels like a moment beyond time. He adds another log to the fire, and I drift back into my internal landscape of thought and imagination.

The ego, the mind, the soul, and consciousness work with the body and the cognitive systems to form imprints, personality, and information. Imagination, intuition, emotion, storylines, and narratives contextualize the imprints. We experience the imprints as thoughts. Thoughts are powerful tools. They are energy. Energy is information. This information spans multiple dimensions and realms to create the experience of all things, all ways. Everything that has been, will be. Everything that will be, has been. Everything is in being in the here and now.

Getting intentional with our thoughts, our words, our actions specifically – day after day – allows us to navigate the potential of the mind. Nightmares, bliss, and everything in between become information. Woven strings come together. Gossamer strands create realities. Energy guides us along a path that strengthens, clarifies, and celebrates the link between the dimensions and realms of being. We can feel it all – the shared chorus of body, energy, mind, soul, and consciousness.

Every thought is an invitation to embrace the wisdom of the realms as they spring forth from currents beyond comprehension. Every thought sparks transformation. Every thought is either a memory, hope for the future, or an anchor to the present. Past, future, and present coexist to build the structures of life and weave the tapestry of reality. We are all, every single one of us, in a forever relationship with our thoughts and the energy of all dimensions of reality.

Opening my eyes, standing to stretch my body, I release a long peaceful breath. He reads his book and embodies a similar sense of ease. Gently touching his hand, I walk to the window.

The snow still falls in big, wet flakes. The moon casts shadows on the white, glistening blanket. Treetops reach up toward the cosmos. No footprints are in sight, only fractals of light that look like diamonds.

The swirling dance of my thoughts that accompanied me up the mountain is all but silent. The stillness of my mind mirrors the stillness of the world beyond the window. An emerging level of the mind bathes my internal landscape – inner peace, true contentment, and Divine ease.

Soon, my head rests on the pillow, and dreams consume my mind in a glimpse of what is becoming.

Thoughts move and shift. Elemental manifestations move and shift. The snows move and shift. Currents of being create our beings. We climb mountains. We travel our inner world. We seek the sacred and find God within.

The next morning, I wake before he does. The fire still smolders in the fireplace as I quietly walk outside to ponder this experience – the lessons of the landscape.

The sun rises over the tree line to the east, and I watch the mist swirl off the snow. The world is revealed again, as it is every morning. Immersed in the present moment through the details of this place, I steep in the meticulous beauty of now.

The light refracts off the ice crystals blanketing the ground, creating rainbows. Snow-covered branches frame the vibrant azure of the sky like a painting graced by the mountain peaks. Drips of already melting snow fall from the incline of the cabin roof. The softness of my vest and the comfort of my boots make me feel safe. The smell of the embers drifting toward the sky is a reminder of warmth. The brisk kiss of the air on my cheeks matches the taste of the chilly air as I breathe deeply.

The sights, sounds, texture, smell, and taste are the details that anchor me to here and now – the external landscape. Closing my eyes and easing into another enormous wave of peace, I notice my heartbeat and my breath. My mind is calm like a trickling mountain stream. These are the anchors of my internal landscape.

The door opens, and his handsome face greets me with a soft, gentle smile. He hands me a cup of coffee. Steam dances in the sunshine just like the mist. Strong hands wrap my shoulders in a wool blanket. The broadness of his chest welcomes me as I lean back into the warmth and sturdiness of his body. The beat of his heart grounds me. We do not say anything.

Refreshed and renewed, this moment, this life, is a creation of the mind – a Divine pulse of being. The cosmic dance received through the perception of these vessels that we call bodies is what it means to be fully alive. We are awake in a dream within a dream.

real or imagined

humanity is precious
each individual
is an aspect of the primal force of creation

together we shift our reality
unveiling profound connections
systems that are Divinely designed

everything and every being
in each lifetime, on each timeline
started in the heart/mind of God

when we open to the flow
of thought
we experience infinite truths

navigate multiple dimensions
find an internal foundation
believe in immaculate potential

absorb and observe
the internal and external
landscapes of being

every aspect of this life
real or imagined
at its core is miraculous

# 8

# AND SO, WE WALKED
## Healing & Listening

---

*"Be fully alive.*
*Be fully aware.*
*Be fully immersed in this human experience."*
*– Intuitive Wisdom*

As I wake from my dreams, she is safe on my chest. I am safe. We are safe.

Today is day five in the hospital. The chrysalis of the birthing center has held and still holds a painful, albeit beautiful, metamorphosis. Breathing recycled air, staring out the window, and longing to feel the warmth of the sun makes me profoundly uncomfortable. Coupled with the complete reprogramming of my biological system, I move through each breath in a haze of anticipation. The trauma of this birthing portal etches its imprint on my energy, my thoughts, and my heart. Healing is necessary. A practice of patience and release to the unknown unfold deep within my subconscious.

As the doctor walks into our room, we stop our conversation and look up expectantly.

"You will need to stay a few more days. Your body needs time," she says with a strained smile.

A tear rolls down my cheek. All I want is to be home.

Rather than recovering in the comfort of our cozy apartment in Northwest Portland, Oregon, we have been here in the hospital, pacing back and forth, waiting for my body to stabilize.

To determine if the medicine is working, every hour, since the diagnosis, the nurses dutifully take my blood pressure. The scratch of the Velcro, the squeeze of the machine, and the thirty-second test provide the numbers that reflect whether my body is healing or regressing. This entire process is nerve-racking and creates a vicious cycle of anxiety, which makes my blood pressure rise more. The discomfort continues to grow.

We were blindsided by this turn of events. Our pregnancy was healthy and beautiful. The early parts of the birth went as expected: fifteen hours of labor at home – easing from tub, to meditation, to listening to my favorite songs on repeat. He came home early from work and held vigil on the gray couch. With him resting when he could, taking the dog for a walk, and making simple food, the entire day was full of ease. Steeping in the currents of allowing, embracing, and listening to the shifts in my body, I felt strong. Excitement and anticipation held us as we encouraged each other through each breath.

The contractions found a rhythm. Then there was a rush of wetness between my legs. She was ready; we were ready. We embarked on a calm walk to the hospital – only five blocks away. Twinkling lights from the winter-holiday decorations that still adorned the storefronts guided each step. Hours at the hospital passed quickly as we moved, breathed, and transitioned into the intensity of labor. Then came the first reroute.

Almost twenty-four hours after my water broke, my body was exhausted, and she became stuck. My vitals and hers were suddenly unstable and fluctuated with each contraction. The doctors suggested alternatives, and while I wanted the birth to be natural, we agreed to the intervention. All we wanted was for both of us to be alive.

After another seven hours of labor, he held her as she took her first breath at 5:38 a.m. This moment was perfect and profound. I birthed our baby. Placing her on my chest, he cut the cord, and we became the bridge of love guiding her first moments on this Earth.

Navigating the bliss of birth is paramount to fully comprehending the human experience. Witnessing the first breath and creating a ceremony of welcoming for the soul starting the earthside journey contextualizes the immaculate beauty of being alive.

For the next two days, we were in complete awe of this portal of birth. Celebrating every sound and consuming every smell, we felt immense joy as it infused every moment – waking and sleeping. We also focused on nurturing my body as she nursed. And he held her for hours as I slept. Novelty and bliss were the currents of energy guiding our new family unit.

Then, the unexpected and another reroute.

Spiking blood pressure and emergency medicine pummeled our bubble of joy. My head throbbed and my body ached as the inflammation increased. My blood pressure rose to near-fatal levels. Intervention was and remains necessary. Had we gone home from the hospital when we were supposed to, I would have collapsed lifeless on the floor of our apartment. God stepped in to guide our path.

In the now moment, as we wait for the medicine to stabilize my internal systems, I hold her tiny body and breathe in her scent. As she nurses gently, I gaze out the window to the world beyond.

Throughout the tempest of this whole situation, skin-to-skin contact has been a lifeline. The neurotransmitters released in all of us through the simple connection of feeling heart to heart have been a necessary salve. In these moments, all of us holding each other, we continue to heal.

Throughout the lived experiences of this life and all lifetimes, we heal the wounds of our bodies and our souls. The individual healing journey guides the healing journey of the collective. True healing is the path toward wholeness. Wholeness guides all beings to holiness. Holiness comes from God within.

As I stare out the window toward the glory of Forest Park, the patterns of the treetops hold my focus as a pair of hawks fly high above the canopy. These trees – the ancient ones, with steadfast devotion – watch generation after generation of humans move through the narratives of being. Along with the trees, the innumerable other ancient beings of our planet guide and guard humanity. They teach us to listen and to feel the dualistic truth of our insignificance and vital importance.

My thoughts drift back to our first weekend here in Oregon.

After one whirlwind year in Seattle, he got a job in Portland,

and our lives were back in boxes. This time, together. With our guard dog, our Subaru, and a zest for adventure, we drove south three hours to what felt like a foreign land of quirk and coffee. We soon realized there was so much more.

Deciding to build our lives between the heart of a volcano and the pulse of the ocean, under the gaze of the giant trees of the old-growth forests, felt aligned on a soul level. The spirits of these lands are fast to initiate the inhabitants. With reverence and dedication, we honored these specific ways of being, and the elemental portals welcomed us.

Just as quickly as we arrived, life shifted again. Days before the test was positive, I felt her in my womb. A bright white light pulsed in my lower belly, indicating the rooting of something greater. A flutter in my energy, a barely perceptible growing body, a portal between souls that was destined, started to weave its golden thread.

After a Monday night yoga class, I stopped by the store and bought a pregnancy test. My growing intuition guided me along the way. When he returned from a night out with friends, I was sitting in shock on our gray couch. Seeing the test in my hands, he went silent.

Then he smiled, "Really?"

We both started to cry – happy tears. In a cloud of immaculate excitement, I soon fell asleep. He stayed awake processing the news. The next day, we felt the timelines shift as we ate bagels across the street. Smiles, disbelief, and unadulterated joy held the moment.

Re-route, reset, shift, and change.

Finding our way in the vast web of being, humans are a transient species on this planet. The trees, the plants, and the ancient spirits are the original inhabitants of this place we call home. Their lives also shift and change, though time and movement are different in their realms.

The original inhabitants were here before we came, and they will be here long after we leave. And yet, in this exact moment, every aspect of aliveness co-creates the fabric of reality. Intricately and intimately existing, each of us is a necessary cell of the living body of this planet.

Participating in the network of life requires courage as we learn to embrace the experience of the unknown and feel the excitement of the new. My relativity in the grand scheme of this planet, of existence, seems so obvious in this moment of birthing my daughter and coming face to face with the potential of my death. The precision of emotion in my human body and remembering of my soul coalesce to create a potent intensity of feeling.

The mantra tumbling through my mind is: "Release to what I cannot see."

My thoughts continue as I watch the trees, as they watch humanity.

Each of us, each object, each quantum particle, every aspect of this dimension and all dimensions, holds the codes of Divine design within the wisdom of the soul. We must remember how to get quiet enough to feel, how to activate our profound capacity to listen, and how to trust the process of healing, to return to the codes of holiness. We are fractals of the Divine. Nothing is random; everything has purpose.

Each moment is a miraculous burst of energy conceived in the heart of it all. The answers are here, patiently waiting for the intersection point of curiosity and intention. Open, close. Up, down. Above, below. Internal, external. Connecting into the spherical truth of what it means to be alive on this planet; feeling into every beautiful aspect of this cosmic intelligence; and trusting that God is charting the navigational map of each lifetime are fundamental to activating our potential.

Amid this portal, this bridge between birth and death, in a sense, I am more alive than ever. At the precipice of living and dying, birthing her, and birthing myself anew, I have activated new levels of comprehension about the vastness of this experience. These days in this hospital room are an initiation of body guided by the soul and guided by God. In the truest sense, it is a process of becoming. Life is a marvel to behold.

As each day slowly rolls on to the next, I find comfort where and when I can. Snuggled into my soft, gray robe and the pillows from home, that he thoughtfully brought back the other day, I study the perfection of her face and map the energy of her field. Her Divine codes are those of the angels. When I tune into her details – the soulful brushstrokes she paints on her canvas of consciousness – they are soft, misty, the color of rose quartz. Her body is small. So, small. And yet, her soul holds the wisdom of thousands of lifetimes. This week in the hospital has gifted us with profound moments of time slowing down.

A whisper falls from my lips, "Everything happens for a reason."

The minutes tick by, and my body begins to find its new level of harmony. We finally receive the news. We get to go home.

Stepping through the doorway of our apartment feels foreign. Conversely, I long to be back in the safety of the birthing wing. There was comfort knowing that a team ready and capable of tending to my body was watching over me.

Now, we are here at home – two creative wanderers who have become parents, medicine, a blood pressure monitor to stave off emergencies and ambulances, and an innocent life bound for human experience. Our dutiful, furry companion who knows something, or someone, has forever changed her life is excited and anxious with our return.

Even with the uneasiness, we are finally home. An exhale releases from my body and tension melts as I fall upon my bed in tears of relief.

The days flow by as friends and neighbors come to visit. Our families book plane tickets to travel to meet our sweet girl. Our new reality is crystallizing.

Still, I am healing. The medicine of these lands is potent, and I feel the forest calling.

Without much of a plan, we – parents, baby, and eager pup – begin a daily devotional practice of walking among and receiving the medicine generously offered by the spirits of the old-growth forests. It is a ritual of respect and a request for healing.

When we tap into the medicine of the trees, we experience cellular and soulful regeneration. Synching to the wisdom of the network of the forest, an almost indescribable transformation happens as our feet hit the trails. Sometimes it is dramatic; sometimes it is subtle.

Always, our microcosmic world does its best to find new ways to survive.

Human bodies are powerful when we align the systems of our internal and external worlds. We are self-healing Divinely designed vessels. The process of healing is cyclical, exactly like the cycles of the cosmos and the rings of the trunks of the trees. Activation and intention are necessary for healing.

And so, we walk. Every day, in all weather, we immerse ourselves in the energy of the trees. Listening to the winds, looking up to the heavens, recalibrating perspective, and activating alignment, we step one foot in front of the other.

Catching a glimpse of movement out of the corner of my eyes – a bird, or squirrel, or something else – reminds me of the cornucopia of beings inhabiting this planet. The red of a berry waits to nourish a fellow forest dweller. Light-codes pierce through the branches in rays of Divine illumination.

Pausing, I hear the song of the forest all around. The rustling of leaves and the swaying of the trees add to the ever-flowing symphony of sounds. Snaps of a branch, the call of the hawk, the cracks of life undulate with the movement of the air. The smell of damp wood, moss, and ferns calms my system. Every detail exists with profound purpose – all at once, or rather at one with. It is a feast for the senses for those willing to indulge.

My feet create a slow rhythm as they land on the soft earth and pine needles. She moves to readjust her new body cradled in her blue cotton baby wrap on my chest. She is hungry and communicating, and I respond to her need for nourishment. I hold her to my chest as we sit on a fallen tree. She receives the life-giving liquid as I receive the life-giving breath of the forest. Closing my eyes, I listen.

The world around us and within us is always talking. Everything everywhere is always talking. An ancient language weaves the conversation for all that can hear. Striving to remember the meaning of this network, my curiosity piques. Chasing answers the way one chases the last bits of light as the sun moves below the horizon. It is elusive and impossible to attain, yet the search for knowing is seductive.

The long hours of contemplation that joined me for so many years feel like a distant memory now that I am a mother. Very rarely am I alone, and I hope I will never truly be alone. Between the long nights of learning to soothe a crying baby and the long days of learning how to build a life, I navigate new questions of being and moments of curiosity. Motherhood – the practice of tending to another human and to myself – creates a channel of deepening awareness.

As my intuition is in a cocoon of its own metamorphosis, my questions are now profound and mundane.

"Why are we alive? What am I going to make for dinner?"

Rather than arriving as words or thoughts, the answers channeled through my intuition now come as a language of feeling.

Listening to her, listening to my own healing body, and listening to the forest through the potent energetic waves of my feeling sense (something beyond the five senses) is now my practice. A demand rises to get quiet enough to feel the ancient language amid the noise of living. Spiraling inward, I arrive at the temple of silence within. In the cave of the heart, the aspect of the soul tends the altar of the temple, which holds the codes of all times, spaces, and realities.

When we get still enough to listen, we feel the vibrational harmony of our hearts sing the song we long to hear. The practice of listening is not about perfection. The practice of listening is one of devotion. Returning over and over, no matter the circumstances, to the Divine temple within is an invitation from the soul.

On my daily walks with the trees as my teachers, I remember new ways to listen. Tuning into the data streaming all around, I learn how to hear the language beyond my ears – the language of feeling.

The conversation goes from one side of the forest to the other, from one forest to the next. Back and forth. Sharing stories and perspectives, the wisdom weaves between the branches and deep within the roots. The birds glide on the tales. The fungi sprout from the memories. Parasymbiotic relationships are all around. Inter-dimensional beings watch the passing seasons and play with the passing of information intertwined with each breath.

As I listen, I feel my heartbeat entrain with my daughter's pulsation. We synchronize to a rhythm that connects all living things to the greater web of the cosmos. Attuning to the pulse of this planet, the crystalline grid, and the great mother – the grandmother of all beings – together, we listen to the ancient truths.

This Earth is conscious and very much alive. She is a being on which we exist knowingly or unknowingly. Each of us carries the narrative of our unique experience of importance. Many of us are unaware of the greater reality. Each human serves a vital role in the health of the whole. The maternal energy of the planet holds all of us with the tender patience of a tired mother doing her best to soothe her children and watch them grow.

Every day, as the light weaves through the branches and the birdsong resets us to our parasympathetic nervous system, we walk. I carry her. He carries her. We emotionally carry each other. We walk and we listen. We walk with one foot in front of the other.

As we walk, I pray for healing. Healing for my body as I continue to recalibrate the experience of birthing her and birthing this new chapter. Healing for her body as she acclimates to the Earth and this life. Healing for him as he integrates the new ways of fatherhood and our dance with death and birth. Healing for all beings everywhere as the dynamics of this planet continue to shift and transform.

Without a pause or a passing of judgement, the voice of God arrives in the wind, the beams of light, and the wisdom of the trees. The messages remind me of the connection of all things: this forest, this life, the cosmos, and all beings everywhere. This is the healing medicine of the forest.

Somewhere out there, red berries are forming, mushrooms are popping, and pairs of hawks are soaring. Somewhere farther out, past other forests, in other homes, babies cry, lovers love, and children play. Somewhere out there, hearts break, and hearts heal. Somewhere out there, cells divide, and stellar life begins. Somewhere out there in the void, immeasurable mysteries await discovery.

Amid it all, I am here, now, feet on the ground, listening to the wind as it moves through the canopy. Hearing God and feeling into the movement of life – to all the universes and back.

## layer by layer

eternal songs of wisdom
can be heard if we listen
sung by the soul
deep in the cavern of our hearts

away from the distractions
ancient chords hum in the realms of the forests
cool dark portals of omniscient presence
vibrations of communication course through the body

an innate language we have long forgotten
something to be felt, not heard
originating in non-physical realities
Divinity of form and frequency

we know how to access art, song, and pulpits
the prophets and the oracles – speaking to the masses
healing now comes from within
between us and ourselves

listening to feel our human evolution
able to receive only a fraction of the actual signature
chords and tones lost in translation
still, the harmonic capacity of humanity is infinite

go beyond the virtual reality as seen through the lens of the eyes
feel what has always been there
waiting to be remembered
shed the discord of the world

layer by layer
learn to listen
to hear the ancient wisdom
the primal harmony of essential existence

# 9

# DIVE INTO COLD WATER

## Emotion & Revelation

---

*"Practice being fully in the experience of living,
so that the energy created and released into the field
is a wave of highest expression."*
– Intuitive Wisdom

There is so much noise colliding with the walls of our home. I am yelling. He is yelling. We are not angry with each other; we are tired and frustrated. Aching with the thought that she might wake up and wail along with us, I try to lower my volume and hope he matches the tone. A deep sigh moves through my body. My eyes close, and my hands fling up around each side of my face – casting an energetic net of protection around my senses.

Our house, which has been lovingly holding us for the past year, is small. Four rooms, a tiny bathroom, and a large magical backyard are all we need. We chose this sweet bungalow in Southeast Portland, primarily because of the giant rhododendrons that grow in the back and the fireplace in the living room. Additional details of the original design add to the charm. A curved front door, porcelain sink, and glass knobs all give character to the space.

Our energy tends to fit perfectly in our home – a simple nest keeping us safe from the outside world. Tonight, however, the rooms feel claustrophobic, and we are bursting with torrents of emotions. While we are comfortable being vulnerable, this exact moment feels overwhelming on layers and levels beyond my capacity of processing.

Many nights, we are like ships passing. He works and comes home. Once he is home, I go to work. We are exhausted. She is beautiful and easy. The throes of young parenthood are complicated and complex. The simplicity and spontaneity that sparked inspiration in the early moments of our relationship are all but gone. And then there are nights like tonight, when we each hit a wall and frustration explodes in a storm of reckoning.

Humans are designed this way – to feel deeply and intensely. We are here in these lifetimes to be unapologetically human, conduits for the raw and potent human experience that we all crave. Something in us resonates with the dichotomy and duality. We desire the spectrum of experience – the good and the bad.

Emotions are how we process the surges of energy. Emotions differentiate us from the rest of the beings on this planet and the multiverse. And still, it does not mean the emotionality of being human is easy. On the contrary, the energy of emotion is extreme; the ache, pain, joy, and ecstasy (and all the vast emotions in between) are necessary to be human.

Our human form, as it processes emotion, is valuable to the evolution of shared universal consciousness. The imprint of emotion infuses the collective field with a range of potential. Our souls choose the human experience for this direct relationship with energy in form. The potential of our emotional energy is paramount. Releasing our full emotional range upon the cosmic intelligence will guide the greater web of being to the next level of expression.

My swirling of frustration continues. Our foundation keeps my worry at bay. Over a decade of friendship and almost two years into parenthood, I trust that we can weather any storm. As we continue to navigate passionate discourse, flares of anger, and flashes of compassion, we ride the waves. The emotions singe. Explosive moments blaze and burn like wildfires or a dragon rising.

A protective instinct arrives. Divine rage takes shape from the cavern of my heart. My soul dons armor to guard the essence of my being, his being, her being, and our future as a family. Internal magic guides the transmutation of this experience. Fires of emotion activate the alchemy of the heart and transform the flames of destruction into the light of illumination and inspiration.

When we embrace each moment, feeling the true current of emotion and stepping into the belief that anything is possible, we become awestruck by the dynamic potential of life. We realize all the ways this life could unfold and all the emotions and reactions that might be felt in each situation. This feels both overwhelming and empowering.

Connection to potential creates a unique way to be in relationship with the future, with the now, and with the reflections on the past. Embracing potential creates a profound shift in how we process the energy of emotion. Rather than locked in fear and limitation, we become inspired by infinite possibilities.

Right now, self-preservation is driving me to get out of the house. Alongside my Divine rage is an urge to run away, far away. To find the looking glass of time and know with certainty how it all happens out. And yet, my heart knows that this, the emotions, and the experience, are necessary, here and now.

Calmly, I tell him that I am done yelling and that I am going for a walk. He scowls but agrees. We need to stop. The energy of our home feels like a kettle at a boil.

As I hit the pavement in a fast-paced walk, the thrashing of my rage begins to soothe toward softer flames. With the lengthening of my breath, I start the practice of calming my mind. Energetic and emotional release continues to flow as my agitated judgement of him, of myself, and our egoic need to escalate the volume and to be right, becomes embers.

Anger is a teacher, and emotion is energy. These truths land as I process the deeper currents of our shared frustration. Pulling the hood of my black raincoat up over my head, pushing my hands into my pockets, I quickly walk into the wet, dark night.

Much of our culture is about business, transactions, and goals. Many of us are trained to suppress emotions and find ways to make it through. We find ourselves not wanting to speak, voice, or even feel at any level beyond what is considered polite. We are told, taught, and funneled into systems that determine our worth based on algorithms and assumed success. Emotions become foreign. We even find it difficult to be happy because we are disconnected from what it is to truly feel.

Instead, we work toward something external – more money, more accolades, more of everything. We move through each moment trying to be better than someone else; sometimes, it is about being better than ourselves. Striving to find satisfaction in the external world, while forgetting the currents of the internal world, leaves us empty, confused, and sometimes disconnected from our original inspirations for being. In our search for perfection and our desperation to quiet the emotional currents, we rob ourselves of the potency of now.

Emotions are energetic currency. Emotions create the depth of experience. All of them. Happy, sad, laughter, tears, joy, despair, trust, doubt, fear, and love are just some of the emotions that create the full range of what makes each moment of life rich and vibrant. The nuance of being acknowledges the beauty in the mess and the truth in the fires of emotion.

My feet continue to carry me through the safe, quiet streets of our neighborhood. As I pass homes, trees, and gardens that soothe me through their simple familiarity, calmness starts to engulf the emotional flames.

Weaving a momentary escape from the current reality, I lean into my imagination. The gateway of my heart transports me in time and place – a practice of bilocation. My awareness is simultaneously in the place of my body and the place of my mind. Both sets of perception converge as the highest expression of my whole being.

I imagine exactly what my energy needs to recalibrate – cold water, space, cosmic light, and wisdom pouring down. Floating through the veils of memory, my mind lands in pre-dawn hours last summer as I sat next to the lake, my save haven in the North Woods.

In this memory, the sky transitioned from dark inky indigo to soft mauve and gentle purples. Like a painting, the colors of the clouds reflected perfectly off the still water. The breeze started to blow, and I watched ripples form on the surface. The light began bouncing along the water, mesmerizing me with the patterns, swirls, and dancing images.

From somewhere within, I felt a call: "Dive."

Although I was hesitant to relinquish the sweatshirt that

warmed my skin against the cold of the air, the courage finally landed. Flinging off the layer, I dove. Swimming under the cleansing sensation until I needed breath, I felt at peace. Surfacing only to take air in, I quickly dove again and swam out into the deeper water. Trusting my body and trusting my breath, I made my way to the small island on the east side of the lake. As I found my footing on the soft, wet sand, I looked up. Sunlight barely came through the trees, and the bald eagle flew high above the water.

I felt the voice again: "Dive."

Back into the water I went, farther and farther, deeper and deeper. My muscles ached, and I turned my body back toward the surface. Catching my breath with a gasp, I stopped swimming and began floating on my back. With my face to the now-brightening sky and my eyes staring into the cerulean abyss, my body felt light and weightless.

And then I saw it in my mind, as clear as a memory, the image of interwoven timelines of realities. Quantum truths presented themselves like paintings in my mind – making so much sense and none at all. I felt at one with the sensations of my body and the Divine revelations coursing through my reality, like I was peeking into the mind of the Creator.

As I floated, I allowed my thoughts to merge with the information pulsing through me from the heavens. My energy became one with the body of a greater being – the planet herself. She held me in the waters of her womb with a Divine force. Beyond the beyond.

All I could do was release into the acceptance of what was happening. The wisdom of the Divine surrounded me like liquid light and radiated within my being. All as one, one as all. We are each so small and so essential. We are not separate, but rather a part of this magnificent planet we call home.

Processing this memory anew, I walk the rain-soaked streets of Southeast Portland and revelations continue to land. The waters of the planet connect to the waters of our bodies. We are terrestrial beings living on a water planet, alive because of the elemental power of water. We have the potential to be cleansed, cleared, and to remember the truth of the waters of reflection. Cold waters hold a power of clarity. The shock surges through the being and forces an activation of consciousness – a pull to get out of the way and to feel the truth.

There are infinite and ancient access points and portals on this planet. Water and light activate all of them. Each point holds essential information for our evolving energy that transforms into the physical through our body. The waters, like emotions, guide the currents of our beings.

Returning to the memory, I try to feel every detail. Flipping over from the floating position, I dove again. Head under water, heart toward the Earth, cleansing my entire form with awareness, and feeling the sensation of freedom, I went deeper and deeper into the lake. It was as if I did not need air – at one with the body of the planet and the Divine mind. Peacefully existing beneath the surface, I flowed with the deeper currents of comprehension.

Surfacing for the breath that I eventually did need, I was awe-struck by the experience. Out of body, in my body, within the body of the planet. This was a Divine activation of oneness and union. The sun had fully risen over the trees, and the light bathed me as I floated, still steeping in the water.

Encountering waves of cosmic truth, I felt everything – individual, collective, planetary, and cosmic energy wove through my form. The micro and macro forever intertwined in the evolution of consciousness. The downloads poured in as if God held the golden pitcher – the water bearer of Divine wisdom.

My attention launches back to the rainy streets as I hear the screeching of tires. Two cars desperately try to avoid each other. Their anger mirrors the emotions that burnt through my home only moments ago. Flashes of fire rise within – not because of the other person but directed there all the same.

Pausing on the sidewalk, I watch the scene. They swerve and miss a near collision. The cars continue, and so do I. Slowing the pace of my stride and taking long, rhythmic breaths, I realize that the antidote to my earlier fire is the memory of diving into cold waters and receiving Divine revelations.

I wonder: "What do I do with these revelations?"

The voice from the center of my heart answers: "Emotions are God guiding us. You are a bridge between the human realm and the Spirit realm. Keep going inward and onward. Teach. They will come. Write to remember your power."

The directions of these words instantly provide context for everything I have experienced up until this point and everything I know I will experience in future moments. Past, present, and future merge into the now moment of multidimensional reality.

We are each constantly in the cycle of becoming, speaking and listening, giving and receiving, living between the portals of birth and death. Our human emotions guide the navigation of our lives. We are receivers of energetic information that expands our perception and shifts our perspective. Emotions, as sources of data, illuminate what we value, what we fear, and what we love. Our consciousness elevates as we integrate the energy of emotion.

Still moving through the rain-soaked streets of my neighborhood, I feel my heart again, this time more softly: "While the memories remind and the future inspires, nothing is more important than the present moment. Everything exists here and now. Emotions are energy generated by the remembering of something greater. The portal to the greatness is forever and always in the here and now. This eternal moment of being is the purpose of being. Lean into the emotions with the essence of remembering who you are."

Emotions, like the harmonious tones, shades, and layers of paint on a canvas, coalesce to create something real. The nuance, the complexity, the vibrancy of life in the third dimension is where we get to feel what it means to be human. No matter how intense experiences become, how fast the emotions flash and burn, belief in the greater truths of being and trust in the multidimensional reality become essential.

My feet guide me back home. A moment of hesitation moves through me as I reach for the handle of our front door. Releasing a long exhale, imagining the calm wisdom of the waters, and the revelations of our connection to the greater being of this planet and to the Divine, I feel at one with everything.

Quiet now holds the space as the door opens, inviting me to

enter. Familiar energy returns to my body, sparked by the details of home – our home. The fire crackles gently in the fireplace. Bookshelves flank the glow with rows of knowledge written on pages. Generations of wisdom are in the time capsules of paper and ink. Pillows on the gray couch and a deep navy-blue rug are objects signifying comfort. Taking off my shoes, I feel the cool wooden floor under my feet.

The memory of the water is fading; so, too, is the fire of the frustration and anger. I feel into the softening. He is there, waiting to hold me as he always has been and always will be. My gaze meets his as we communicate in silence – furrowed brows and half-smiles. We hold each other tightly as my head nestles perfectly under his chin, feeling the rhythm of his breath and the beat of his heart. We never mean for the energy to get so intense; yet the cleansing is always necessary. We are the ones for whom the other holds this sacred relationship.

The tears flow as we share the energy of release. The ignition of emotion and the memory of Divine waters cracked something within me, and now the golden light of love is filling the gap. Emotion, revelation, and the cycle of becoming guide each moment, each breath.

He decides to head out for a walk as he is reassured that we are both okay. I am okay. He is okay. We are okay.

As he leaves through the back door, I check that she is still sleeping. Then, I sit down with a pen in my hand. Writing to connect, I receive more revelations of my heart, the wisdom of the Divine, and the cosmic truths of being – eternally synchronizing with the elevated comprehension of all there ever has been and all there ever will be.

Pouring many words onto the page, these are the first phrases that come: "As the body relaxes, the breath moves. As the breath moves, the body relaxes. The ticking clock of our co-created reality exists because of self, others, and God. Emotions are sacred. Purpose is guided. We are each essential. All swirling in the cosmos. Until the moment this iteration of energetic form is done, and the cycle starts again."

## a world unknown

this world is full of complexity
every facet unwinding, swirling, drifting
each moment connecting, weaving, guiding

a single branch falls from the tree
traveling around the bends of the river
finding the mouth of the ocean

storms pummel its bark until it is no longer what it was
fish bite into its flesh
calm seas provide a bed of rest

the sun shines its rays down upon the singular form
all the while, a story is written
years pass and the identity is not the one it once was

different from when it was connected to its home
the tree rooted deeply in the ground
no, it has found new shape

morphed into a new entity all its own
as the winds kick up strong waves, the sky darkens
the clouds cast shadows

the moon becomes desperate to find the wood
floating on the depths
of this vast mysterious place

unaware that it is creating
the very movement causing
the waters to hide its muse

no longer a branch
instead, a story book
charting miles of adventure

existing in a world unknown
content in a world unknown
allowing for the unknown to become known

thinking back on the moment
that everything shifted
lightning strikes, cracking open possibility

the branch far from its origin
just like all of us
we are each a thread in this cosmic fabric

essential like each drop of the ocean
each bead of moonlight
riding the swells of being

we find ourselves
exactly where
we are intended to be

# 10

# TIDES OF BEING

## Adventure & Consciousness

---

*"Listen to the siren song of the heart.*
*All aspects of experience lead to the next.*
*We are in the infinite spiral and dance with God."*
– Intuitive Wisdom

Sitting comfortably on the gray couch in our living room, he recounts the tale of his adventure. Reflecting that the most profound aspect of his hike – his personal quest – was the experience of being absolutely alone and realizing how much life was still around. Hiking solo between the Pacific Ocean and the Olympic National Forest for six days required preparation and perseverance.

There were moments when he felt so deeply vulnerable, and yet he continued. Cove after cove, with each step, he woke up to a new way of thinking, being, and existing. He explored a new paradigm of adventure in a novel yet ancient landscape. Emerging from transient states and completing the journey, he achieved freedom and liberation from the confines of his ego.

Needless to say, he has changed. He arrived back to our bungalow with an energy and cadence of a new way of being – smelling like the pine of the forest and the salt of the sea.

He explains how time on the coast is measured by the flow of the tides, not told by the ticking of a clock. Like all sacred shifts of awareness, time falls away.

Time is a construct, not linear but cyclical, just like the multiverse. Time expands and contracts. Minutes can feel like hours, hours like seconds. Time is relative. Time as a creation of the human society is not the same as the time of the tides. When we release the construct of time, planetary consciousness becomes obvious as the individual merges with the sacred rhythms. Everything is forever in the cycle of evolution. By embracing these greater cycles of being, we recognize that we exist within layered realities – fractals of one another.

When living in union with the rhythm of the ocean, the roar of the wind, and releasing from the construct of time, it becomes apparent that intelligence is not reserved simply for humans. This is a truth humanity has been unveiling for eons. The plants, animals, and technology that cohabit this planet all hold essential and necessary signatures of intelligence. These signatures coalesce to support the collective energy of the planet.

This truth sank deep into his bones when he investigated the paw prints that covered his camp one morning. Another being, not human, had come to visit. He felt a connection on a soul level.

He asked himself: "Am I really seeing what I think I'm seeing? What is real? Is this a dream?"

Knowing he was being watched while he slept roused him into a new awareness and perception. Life and conscious beings are all around. Looking toward the sky, he saw the dance of consciousness in the clouds, which are always rolling and moving, just like the tides. He felt so small and also so essential. His pulse added to the vibrations of the landscape.

The next day, as he meditated within a cave only accessible because the tide was low, he looked out at the crashing waves and thought: "I am the only one creating the drama. The anxiety, emotions, and charge are coming from my thoughts. The rest of the landscape exists as a sacred flow of being."

In that moment, a revelation landed in his heart, and he shares it with me now.

"This world is a stage. The action is the weather, the people, the ecosystems – micro and macro. Rain and storms add to the climax. In some places of the world, not a drop of water falls for weeks. Along the coast, the water pours from the sky as an emanation from heaven. The sun is always there, witnessing and watching the spectacle – no matter who is calling the scene change."

So much is beyond our control – from visiting animals in the darkness of night, to the clouds, the tides, and the cosmos. Watching the magical shifts and changes of the natural flow of life connects us to the organic and inorganic realities of our contemporary life. Planes fly by, as do the birds.

He continues recollecting the moments of his journey, and details emerge with fantastic specificity: other coastal cave meditations, barnacled boots, choreographing his movements to the metronome of the tides, reading and re-reading the same Eastern philosophy text over and over. The crystallized experiences were truly profound.

As I listen, a memory of our family road trip home from the lake last summer lands in my mind. This memory is spurred by how much he has changed, how much he has evolved.

They were both asleep. She was in her car seat, head gently leaning to the right. His hat was drawn over his eyes so that I could only see his beard. Both of them were breathing rhythmically and smoothly. The night before, he barely slept. The notion of realms within realms turned on his heart. In conversation and community with dear friends in Bozeman, Montana, we explored deep topics: the potential of this life, the convergence of multiple timelines, the concept of time, consciousness, and the layers, levels, and vastness of being. Yearning to be in a state of soulful knowing, we navigated the ebb and the flow.

Until that evening, his unique path of spiritual curiosity so perfectly intertwined with mine. For years, we have practiced meditation and yoga, communed with elevated ways of being, and invited curious thoughts about the meaning of life. And yet, after the conversation with our friends, he seemed more confused and overwhelmed as the true codes of wisdom still felt elusive to him.

While driving west on Interstate 90, in the hours before sunrise, I felt a profound alignment in my being. A true contrast and opposition to where his energy was hovering. Figuratively, he and I were at a crossroads. My wisdom expanded in my field of awareness, and his remained hidden in the cave of his heart. We were indeed journeying together, but as of this moment, we began taking different paths.

The passing white dashes that marked the center of the highway were hypnotic, and I slipped into my own activation. There was no traffic, just mile after mile of incalculable space and the magic of the landscape. The pre-dawn light cast shadows from the mountains onto the field as the world was between moments of sleeping and waking. The cows in the pasture were unaware of the drama of humanity.

My mind drifted from here to there as I thought about all the people who had driven this road. The humans who lived on these plains long before there were roads. The geological history in the mountains and rocks. How grand this space felt and how tiny it is in comparison to the whole of the planet and the cosmos. And again, as always, I suppose, I thought about our interconnected web of being and shared field of consciousness.

An uplevel of information entered my inner monologue. It was as if the mountains began speaking, and all I had to do was listen.

Consciousness is part of the higher dimensions and is within us. Shared consciousness is the sacred intelligence that wraps, moves, and inhabits every aspect of matter and every aspect of the immaterial. Consciousness as an energy field is woven into every blade of grass, every being, every mountain peak, and each aspect of the cosmic landscape. Collective and individual consciousness are fractals of the shared consciousness. The evolution of consciousness is the purpose of the human experience. Consciousness evolves when we evolve, and as we evolve, we arrive at new levels of intelligence.

This download came from the mountains, the light, the web of being, and the openness of my heart. Feeling at one with the pulse and beat of aliveness, my entire system upgraded its code of wisdom. My intuition was flowing anew. Everything within me shifted into a new level of knowing – all while holding space for where he was hovering.

Pulling into the gas station, I merged with signs of human life and the smell of fresh brewed coffee. He started to rouse and smiled as if to say thank you for driving. Essential transformation had begun to take place in the realms beyond time, each of us with our own unique expression. It felt like lifetimes had passed, even though it had only been a few hours. The relativity of time.

Since that conversation last summer, he has been striving to unlock the inner knowing of past and future selves and has been engaging within himself a precise dance of thought, still learning where to step and when.

Shifting my attention back to the now moment, I listen intently as he continues sharing, talking, and detailing what seems like one of his most profound experiences of upgrading and upleveling. He allows me to witness, through the gateway of his journey, the blossoming of his heart. His adventure on the coast taught him the dance steps and he is now nimble in the movements of thought and being. I am open to receive and honored to share this space.

Adventure is a concept and a feeling. Life itself is the greatest adventure. The soul chooses to leave the comforts of the Spirit realm to journey into the density and duality of the human experience. Soul-led willingness mirrors our human capacity for courage. Bravery guides our immersion into the complexity of being and stays present through it all. From a place beyond time, we learn to live within its construct.

The fragility of our condition and the miraculous perfection of what it means to be human are among the reasons we chose to incarnate on Earth. Our souls desire to experience the nuance, the duality, the trials and tribulations, the high highs and low lows.

Metamorphosis of our shared consciousness requires bravery, strength, and power – both human and soul. Activating the heart requires immense courage. Humans move through life moment by moment – page by page – navigating the tides of our being. Courage is required to go into the unknown and face the fear, where we discover gateways to sacred ways of being that span lifetimes and timelines. Into the cave, through the cave, and out of the cave to arrive at a more profound knowing. Just like the mist of the sky and the rhythm of the ocean, there is an intangible quality to the spiritual journey.

Looking around, I absorb the details of our home – the plants hanging in the window, the records next to the record player, the light cast by candles on the mantle. Pulling a soft, cream wool blanket up to my chin, I continue to listen to all he has to share. An honest recognition lands in my being: *I am no longer who I was. And neither is he.* We have been and continue to do the dance of wisdom and evolution. We are accepting what arrives in our hearts – our activated hearts.

The kettle on the stove begins to whistle. Walking toward the kitchen and grabbing a pair of socks from the unfolded pile of laundry in the corner of our living room, I slip them on to protect my feet from the cold linoleum floor. Moving the kettle from the burner, I take down two cups. They are handmade artifacts we bought at a farmers' market when we lived in Seattle. Slipping the tea bags into the mugs, I slowly start to pour the liquid into the vessels. The swirls of the steam move and match the account of the mist along the coast.

He is pensive and far off in his thoughts as I hand him the cup of tea. Here we are again, sitting on the same gray couch that has traveled with us from home to home. The same couch we sat on together when I told him we were pregnant. It is an anchoring part of our lives, which is now worn and loved. Just like each other.

Together, we share a moment of sacred silence. Each of us is reflecting on the consciousness and the intelligence of all things, the transformational journey of human and soul, and feeling into the activated heart that remembers the cosmic truths and holds space for love – our love. His desire to hold the elevated energy and perspective of the ocean is palpable. The mountains speak to me through my memories and reflections. The tides speak to him through his memories and reflections.

The drumbeat of daily life comes back into our perception, with the rising challenge of integrating his adventure, alongside my individual evolution.

Integration is the intentional embodiment of the troves of wisdom that exist in all dimensions and realms. Integration is the part of the process when we reflect, contemplate, and feel the benefits of our transformations. When we integrate experiences into our physical beings, we upgrade our systems to operate in new ways. It is one thing to learn the knowledge, read the books, take the trips; it is something entirely different when we apply the wisdom.

On a fundamental level, we strive to hold the ancient truths of this planet and the vital wisdom we feel flowing in the very fibers of our beings. Whether consciously or unconsciously, we listen to the whispers of our souls heard in the mists of the sea and the shadows of the mountains. Everyone can find the courage to hold space for the spiritual journey of evolution. The sacred energy of eternal unfolding is found in every moment and in everything.

Locking directly into his piercing blue eyes, I say, "One breath at a time. We can only ever live one breath, one step at a time."

As we continue to hold each other's gaze, time feels like it is standing still. In a way it is – everything is relative. Our hearts hum with eternal truths. Evolution is the adventure of existing one breath after another, until we stop and transition back into the field of consciousness guiding us all.

## step through the gateway

above it all, it is all the same
light shines through the rising and falling of form

varying densities, unifying space
different rhythms and similar cadence

the world embraced in a wisdom
arriving from beyond

our superficial layer of thinking
transforms with aligned action

limiting views keep us reactive
to the protection of things

warring for reasons that contradict reason
both internally and externally

evolving as we do, or so we can
seeking remains of utmost importance

innate gnosis is the driver
unlocking layers of knowing, doing, creating

one beautiful aspect of humanity – our ingenuity
reveals the perspective of the cosmos

aligning us to the intersection points of existence
expanding, returning, and shifting eternally

beings of light receive a direct transmission from the Creator
look to the sky and wonder

look at the face of a beloved and see
this moment is pure

innocence forever encapsulated
in the beauty of now

communion with the Divine
exists exactly here

step through the gateway
feel beyond the constructs of this world

there is no justification for division
stay with the tone, the calling

there is a tide of existence
a rise and a fall

shedding and mutations
evolution is necessary

our unique spectrum of experiences
adds to the multiverse of being

rest with ease
stabilize in all iterations of self

# 11

# MERGER OF THE REALMS
## Belief & Meditation

---

*"Hold awareness for all beings everywhere.*
*There are portals of knowing in all moments.*
*Remember how to receive."*
*– Intuitive Wisdom*

Today is wet and cold. Something I have grown accustomed to during late autumn visits to Ecola State Park. The dampness of the moss, as it drapes down from the trees, is calming and mysterious. The energy of the forest, as it meets the sands of the beach, is the medicine I seek. Elemental details hold space for me to move into my reflections and contemplations.

Winding roads navigate through the towering pines, as I imagine fairies and magical creatures darting between the trees. Years ago, I dreamed of making my way to the ocean. What I did not know was that the ocean would become a confidant, a friend.

My daughter is with me, as she has been nearly every day since she was born. We share, and will always share, a bond that transcends time.

During a profound meditation a year after her birth, I received confirmation of our soul connection. A trusted healer recommended a ceremony called bone closing. During the ceremony, the body of the mother is gently and intentionally wrapped in sacred fabric, creating a safe space to release any tension still existing in her form.

In my bone-closing ceremony, I listened to the healing sounds of the crystal singing bowls and the voice of my healer. My body drifted into a blissful space of receiving. I sensed my energy shifting and moving through the layers of consciousness toward the realms beyond. Part of my soul ventured deeper as it journeyed through the threshold where the Spirit realm meets the human realm, while another part remained grounded within my body.

Steeped in sacred, meditative energy, I landed back in the moment of her birth. Angels and what felt like beings of golden light greeted and imbued me with Divine knowing. Profound healing spiraled through me as I remembered that her soul chose to arrive in the exact way she arrived.

More wisdom activated in my mind, my heart. Her soul is here to guide me through profound layers of healing. My soul is here to guide her into what it means to be human. Together, we are here to embody evolved levels of intuition, knowing, and remembering.

After revisiting the moment of her birth, my healer held space for me to deepen my meditation in silence. In my mind, the scene changed (like in a dream) and suddenly I was watching from above. The vision that unfolded before me was the weekend my husband and I spent in Paris during our semester abroad. We casually shared breakfast at the tabac across the street from the hostel – a simple moment of everyday being.

As I hovered in my mind above the scene, I felt like a spectator watching the movie of my own life. Then I noticed that I was next to our daughter's soul. She was unaware of me. Watching her, as she was watching us, as we were watching each other, showed me that all three of us are intricately linked in the journey of our souls.

Deep in the meditation, a knowing landed in my awareness: *this was the moment when she chose us as parents.* The experience of this meditation reminded me of something I have long believed. Souls choose each other. Souls guide each other into, through, and toward the higher levels of consciousness. We choose each other for the experience of love, forgiveness, and soul-led growth.

The meditation continued. The scene of my daughter choosing us and watching us from above zoomed out. Again, the images changed quickly. My soul traveled my consciousness and landed in space, where I heard a voice.

An angelic voice said: "Her brother is waiting, but there is no rush. He is ready when you are."

Eventually, with my human senses, I heard the voice of my human healer. She was luring me back into my body and into the human realm.

Waking up from the meditation, unwrapping from the sacred fabric, rolling my shoulders, and reorienting to my home, I said to my healer, "You won't believe what I just experienced."

She said with a knowing smile, "I might! Write it down, so you do not forget."

On some level of knowing, our interwoven reality begins to make sense. These visions, as clear as dreams and as real as the waking world, hold such meaningful truth. The path of remembering expands our ability to believe in the infinite – to genuinely believe in what we cannot see. What we call mystical and magical, tones that harmonize our being with the portals of higher knowing, are in fact very real.

Here on the beach, wrapped now in sweatshirts, raincoats, and scarves, a world away from that moment and those visions, I reflect on the wisdom received during that meditation. The song humming in the memories of my soul reminds me that infinite worlds exist and overlap. Innumerable strands of energy move through the gateways of our human hearts – the merger of the realms. Believing in the unbelievable and impossible guides us to hear the melody. All aspects of being are held in the eternal golden orb of the multiverse.

And also, we are deeply connected to this planet, our chosen timelines, and the immaculate beings with whom we have chosen to create a life. All of us, in this together.

Under the gray sky and misty clouds, her small body – full of curiosity, observation, and a zest for life – runs rapidly toward the waves. Still linked to the realms beyond and fascinated with rediscovering this dimension and world, wisdom pours through her as it always will.

Stopping just short of the water, I reach out for her hand. Staring down at her face, I am mesmerized by her beauty. Her long lashes and hazel eyes make her look properly angelic. Many people comment on this quality of hers. A woman in the grocery store the other day spoke to her in a foreign language, and she nodded as if she understood.

The woman then looked up to me and said, "I read people's energy, and this little one is here to set an example of the potential of the evolved human. She comes from the stars."

At that moment in the store, I was not sure what it meant, but I agreed. In the now moment, I pick her up, spin her around, and feel her magic flow. She laughs and throws her head up to the sky in joyful abandon.

"Mama, look!" she says in her sweet voice as she points down the beach toward a flock of gulls.

Steadying herself on the sand, she starts running again. She is so alive – so fully alive.

Afternoons like this allow me to reset. Our life is overflowing and abundant. Almost daily, I am at the yoga studio, a bustling community in the Pearl District, the heart of Portland, Oregon. Teaching is and always has been fulfilling and stimulating. Guiding bodies through the practice of movement, meditation, and breath inspires me. Sharing my distillation of ancient teachings and wisdom with groups of curious, impassioned, and seeking souls activates my voice.

Through the pathways of teaching, my multidimensional capabilities – channeling and transmitting in real time – are coming online in potent ways. Feeling energy, reading auric fields, and knowing the emotional memories of the people in the room without speaking, transport me into a new level of holding space and guiding students.

Many days, the curious characters and beings who sometimes come to class make me smile about the multiple personalities that coexist on this planet. The constant stream of input into my system is exhilarating. Sometimes, though, it leaves me exhausted. Often, on days when I feel overstimulated, we retreat to the ocean and the old-growth forest. The ancient portals of this mysterious landscape reorient and regulate my being.

My attention shifts as her little hand tugs at mine.

"Mama, I am hungry," she shares.

The square, green blanket that goes with us on most outings offers the perfect table for our picnics. Setting our space far up the beach, away from the waves and other people, I lay out snacks and water. She begins playing with rocks, stacking them and making shapes of circles and hearts. Our sweet dog – our guardian and companion – is with us, resting gently on the sand. We are safe; all is well.

Feeling a more potent tug from my soul asking me to tune in, I lie on the beach and connect with the pulse of the ocean. Closing my eyes for a moment, I travel again through the portal of my mind and land in a memory of a vision from another sacred ceremony years ago at the yoga studio where I worked in Washington, D.C.

In that ceremony, we were dancing, spinning, and embracing ecstatic movement. The teacher then guided us to drop down on the ground and allow our minds to travel. Slipping instantaneously into a deep meditation, I saw a vivid vision.

Experiencing through my mind, I felt my body on wet, cold ground. Snow surrounded me. The nose of a stag nudged me to wake up. The antlers were eight points, and the energy was gentle, yet fierce. Telepathically, he invited me to ride through the woods. Mounting his strong back, I was immediately at one with what felt like a mythical energy.

We rode through the forest until we arrived at a cottage. Dismounting, I began to investigate the scene. Through the window, I could see myself inside by the fire. I was not the young female body that I currently am. I was an older male with many years of wisdom drawn on my face – a version of myself from another realm and another lifetime.

As I looked more closely at the details of the space, I knew exactly where I was. It was a cabin where I had lived for years during another incarnation. Feeling myself warp into the body of the man, I could hear the fire and feel its warmth. Beyond the doors, demons banged and trolls clamored. Sitting still, I remained peaceful as I listened to the flames. Eventually, the demons stopped, and all was quiet. Wisdom poured from every inch of my body, and I felt like I was glowing.

Still in the vision, in this scene beyond the time and space of our world, I stood up in front of the fireplace. There was immense warmth and calm. As I walked through the portal of the door, I transitioned again to the size of a little girl tiptoeing through the now-sleeping monsters. Walking outside the cabin, bare feet on the soft, white ground, I felt the coldness of the snow and the clarity of the winter air. I mounted the stag once again, and we galloped off into the forest. The vision dissolved, and the meditation ended.

In my current reality, I open my eyes and see the bright blue of the Pacific sky. Mere moments have passed. Such is the time warp of the mind. Gone for hours in memory and only seconds in waking reality, this is how we experience the merger of the realms.

The mists of the ocean are moving, and I hear my daughter's voice.

She taps my arm and calls to me, "Mama. Mama."

She begins climbing onto my chest and snuggling in. Scooping her up, I hold her close to feel her heartbeat and warmth. She wiggles off and runs down the beach toward her preferred climbing rock. Navigating the bumpy surface while singing a song from her imagination, she smiles with delight. Gathering our things, I reflect on these visions and memories.

We are not simply awake or asleep. We are moving through a constant gradation of conscious awareness. Magic is found when we maneuver the mind and see the realms beyond the perception of the senses. We can access the liminal space between the waking world and the dream world, the multiverse and the planet, the Spirit realm and the human realm. As our consciousness evolves and our souls remember, we are invited to travel with rhythmic oscillation between all layers and levels of reality.

Learning to hold awareness, assimilate within, and calibrate multiple dimensions is part of the initiation of being. Finding stability after the expansion is the experience of returning to center, to the mid-line, to the cave within, where the soul and human rest in a loving, knowing embrace. Our multidimensional experience unveils the reservoir of creation.

The merger of the realms is where time does not exist as we think of time in our human world, where reality is flexible and malleable, where we embrace dynamic truths of healing, and prepare for the shifts to come. Every night when we fall asleep and dream, we experience the merger of the realms, whether or not we remember upon waking. When we look at the horizon, we see that every drop of water eventually merges with the great body of the ocean. All is connected; everything carries the sacred codes of all incarnations.

The wet sand underfoot is familiar and soothing. Our dog comes along dutifully. Taking my time, mindful not to rush, I listen intently to the crashing of the waves and the sound of the wind – the song of the ocean.

My daughter climbs down the rock and grabs my hand. Now, we walk together. As we near the other side of the cove, we head away from the water and scramble over driftwood and stones to make our way to the stairs. Climbing up and off the wet sands, passing through the parking lot, we settle into our Subaru, quiet and calm.

As I drive slowly out of the parking lot, my mind drifts again to the memories of my meditations and visions – portals to other realms and dimensions. An immense amount of peace floods my being as I align with the greater ways of being. We all experience lifetimes within lifetimes and dreams within dreams. The mystical and magical energy of life embraces all of us with the sweetness of Divine wisdom.

The road winds and curves around the animated ancient trees and giant ferns. She is sweetly singing in her car seat. Enchantment inhabits this part of the forest. Even with my eyes open, I feel like we are moving through the realms into another world. A knowing weaves through the trees. The network of ancient guardians continues to hold space for humanity, despite it all.

Suddenly, I brake hard. Crossing over our path, or maybe we are crossing over theirs, a herd of elk passes directly in front of us. The majestic ancestors know every drop of mist, every turn of the roots, and every trail between the trees. They sing the songs of the ancient ways as they bugle between the towering trunks.

Knowing very well what a herd of elk could do if they decided to move in unison, I inch forward cautiously as they have the power in this situation. They hold their ground and I stop the car again. We all wait and watch.

Her singing quiets as she looks out the window.

"Mama, look!" she exclaims in amazement.

Our guard dog is on high alert, and yet she is also quiet. Not barking, only watching. We are all frozen in what seems to be an eternal moment of being.

Slowly the bull moves. And then, as if they understand his thoughts, the herd parts, allowing enough space for our car to pass. We crawl through the pack, noticing more and more elk as my eyes adjust to the beings camouflaged by the landscape. Pausing again, I assess the safety and distance between the car and the herd. Locking eyes with the bull, for a moment, we hold each other's gaze.

The soul illuminating the eyes feels like the same soul of the stag I encountered in my vision many years ago.

Without uttering a sound, I send the thought: "Thank you."

Another car starts coming in our direction. The herd around me disappears into the forest. As I drive forward, I look through the rearview mirror; they are gone completely into the mist and the trees.

Overwhelmed and having trouble believing this actually happened – in real time, in this realm, this world, and reality – I park the car by the ranger's station just up the road. For a moment, I question if I am imagining the whole scene, if this is a dream, or if I am again in a meditation.

And then I hear her say, "Mama, did you see that? Wow."

The dog starts barking, and I am brought fully back into the human dimension – where in fact, this actually did happen. Picking up the phone to call him, I know I must share our experience before I convince myself that it was not real.

He calmly receives the story, the details, the narrative of memories, meditations, guides, and guardians. Not doubting for a moment the portals of these lands, he confirms the power of the ocean, the forest, the ancient beings, and sacred guardians. He knows them well, and now I do too.

As I drive, she quickly falls asleep. Drifting into a space of reflection and integration, receiving all that has been, and opening to all that is, I feel the beat of evolution.

They – the guardians of the wisdom, the spirit guides, the ancient ones, the ones existing in the realms beyond – are with us always. They are the ones who open the gateways and invite us to travel between the realms.

Feeling their voices, I hear them say: "May you experience all that is needed for the evolution and transformation of Spirit."

## imagination is the antidote

focus the energy on the eternal now
activate the innate portal of wisdom

the guardians guide us
to what we all know to be true

release the desire to make it make sense
feel what the soul sees and knows

follow the call of the ancient truths
and the realms and dimensions beyond

the tides flow and the forests grow
we are here to evolve our beliefs

strand by strand, link by link
unweave and unwind

imagination is the antidote
to the contemporary way of living

everything is possible
follow the pathways of remembering

the journeys, the visions, the dreams
the multiple realities that are in fact actually happening

# 12

# THE SONG OF LOVE

## Birth & Surrender

---

*"There is so much more to all of this.*
*Fragility and beauty exist each moment of being alive.*
*Appreciate all of it."*
*– Intuitive Wisdom*

The experience of birth is both unique and unifying. We each are born through a physical portal, the womb of a mother. Genetically and soulfully coded, every single human holds immense amounts of physical and metaphysical information. Innumerable orders of processes ensue to create a life – from the Spirit realm to the earth-bound reality.

Every mother who has carried a child in her womb knows about the fragility of this process. Cells upon cells divide, expand, and grow in predetermined ways, based on a core code at the center of each individual body and soul. Contracts for each lifetime are agreed upon in the realms beyond activating with each phase of the physical process. The mother surrenders as she is the only vessel in which this Divine experience unfolds.

Each morning, day, and night, the mother feels an indescribable connection to the child. Doing her best to ensure their survival, navigating the fluctuating hormones, and feeling the moment the soul lands in the body requires a monumental amount of energy.

For the last nine months, this is exactly what I have been doing: responding to my primal intuition all while tending to my daughter, our life, my responsibilities, and my other roles of this human experience.

Our newest member, our son, has been ready to arrive for weeks. Every night for the last month, I experienced prodromal labor, which is bouts of contractions that start and then stop, producing no active results.

Last week, my blood pressure began to fluctuate. Paying attention to the false labor and rising blood pressure, my doctor felt like my system might again be getting unstable. To avoid emergency decisions, we chose a date for delivery at the hospital.

As we load the bags into the car, my womb feels heavy. I am wearing a long, flowing white linen dress, and the summer air is hot and sticky. With kisses, hugs, and reassurances, we bid farewell to our daughter. My mother, having just arrived to care for our sweet girl, holds me and looks into my eyes with a silent blessing. Scratching the ears of our dog, with a few last kisses on her nose, we place the final bag for our altar – the sacred space we intend to create to welcome him earthside – into the car.

My energy is trepidatious and also calm. Something rises in my chest and moves up and down my spine as we pull away. It is a knowing that, when we return, we will not be the same – our family is transforming.

Pregnancy and birth are so fragile and so beautiful. When multiple souls are involved in an intersection moment of human reality, the experience does not belong to only one person. An immense amount of strength is required to move with all the possibilities and potential outcomes. The first breath, the first meeting, and the acceptance of the contracts from the higher realms all crystallize the lifetime. In this portal, individual energy merges or dissolves. The experience of birth creates an anchor point on the journey of the soul.

As we arrive back to the birthing wing at the hospital in Northwest Portland, they guide us to a different room. The view still overlooks Forest Park and the ancient trees. My husband, my partner, the blue eyes that ease my energy, is with me through every breath. Holding my hand, holding my gaze, and reassuring every decision, his steadfastness never wavers.

Twelve hours in, something feels out of alignment. Moving my body, singing the songs, and calming my system, I breathe deeply. During the pregnancy, I did a particular yoga practice to prepare me for this moment. Dropping into specific postures, mantras, and hypnotic mindfulness, I hope they will shift the trajectory.

Something, however, is not right. Listening inward to the intelligence of my womb, an answer rises. The baby is stuck, and everything is about to change. On some level, throughout this whole pregnancy, I knew that this portal of birth would reprogram me forever.

Months ago, as I stood at the kitchen sink rubbing my growing belly, I had a vision. My precognitive knowing has been landing with more accuracy for years. Seeing, feeling, or knowing events before they come into being – clairvoyance – is something I am learning to navigate. This vision, this flash of the future, felt precise. The surety of the energy was crystallized and definitive. The scene of his birth flashed in my mind, and I saw the cut in my abdomen.

At that moment of feeling the future, I grabbed the counter to steady myself. As I glanced over at the knives in the knife block, the precognitive images made me shudder. This vision was a moment of my future and one I did not want to experience.

While I arrived in the world via cesarean, I wanted to bring him into this dimension through the birth canal. The inner monologue of failure, if I was unable to provide that gateway, consumed my thoughts. So, I spent months visualizing the powerful birth I desired and read about. I was fixated on a natural, flowing, graceful, primal birth guided by breath and surrender.

And yet, from the moment of that premonition to this moment now, I knew on some level that my ego was not in control of how this would unfold.

Intuitive and precognitive knowing guide us to surrender to the choices of the soul, even when the human ego resists. This is not easy. Surrender is not about giving up. It is the aligned action necessary to claim the power of belief in the unseen and trust what our human ego cannot fully comprehend. Surrender allows for union with, rather than a resistance against, the chosen timeline. Surrender requires that we claim our power from a higher perspective.

On the practical side of things, modern medicine is doing its best. The doctors try to move him inside of me. They monitor his heartbeat and mine.

"The baby might move; let's give it a little longer. Keep breathing. Try to relax," my doctor says with a hopeful tone.

My eyes close as I sway, move, and release. My eyes open to find his steady blue eyes sitting next to me. We take long, rhythmic breaths, together.

Eventually, our son's vitals are no longer stable. The doctors and nurses come into the room. Our son needs to be earthside, and I need to feel his body in my arms. We are all ready for him to take his first breath. We must decide what to do next.

The unexplained and unexpected are uncomfortable. In moments of unknown, discernment is essential. Discernment is our capacity to hold the possibilities of all timelines and move forward in alignment with our soul wisdom. Discernment is a radical act of self-preservation in the face of uncertainty. When someone asks us to follow them, or tells us to do something, we must ask ourselves why, and does this resonate with our higher knowing? This internal inquiry – also known as tuning in – is an intimate dialogue between our human and our soul.

As we take aligned action and prepare for the next steps of this portal of birth, my eyes close again and I synchronize into one of the most potent channels of intuitive communication. This elevated direct channel is with my group of guides.

Our first conscious encounter was months ago during a meditation early in the pregnancy. Their energy was above, below, within, and surrounding my field of awareness. Holding council high above the canopy of the atmosphere – in a different dimension – they were magnificent and wise. Their energy penetrated my consciousness as blue light, like guardian angels. They are magnetic, electric, and radiant beings, who are always and forever guiding, guarding, and protecting my soul journey.

In the meditation, they answered many questions about the portal of birth and our individual human power to make decisions as they relate to the decisions of the soul. Human ego, bodies, and souls all work together to determine the evolving path of each incarnation. Timelines shift and change, and yet the soul will always experience what it needs to experience in each lifetime.

Now, my group of guides have joined me in this birthing room. Desperate to find another way to bring him into the world, I begin to communicate with them.

Through my thoughts, I ask: "Is this the only way? I need to know that this is the only way."

They whisper in my heart: "You are safe. Surrender."

Telepathically, they share more information about the purpose of this portal and the process of the cesarean. Through their guidance, I learn that he has chosen this timeline. As I remember this soul decision, I know I must surrender. My body relaxes, my breath flows, and my ego finally releases.

The doctors ask if we consent to the cesarean, and we confirm. The team around me prepares my body for surgery. Everything goes quiet in my mind.

A part of my soul leaves my body, flowing with my consciousness, to join my guides holding vigil in the dimensions beyond. I am not fully in my body. I am not fully gone. Like in my visions and my dreams, I witness from somewhere else.

For a moment, physical discomfort brings me back into my body, and I find my human voice. The doctors make some adjustments, and part of me again flows out of my body.

From above, I see my husband next to me, his face taut with worry. He furrows his brow, sets his jaw, and tenderly holds my hand. The part of my soul that is above watches them cut my abdomen and remove my son from my body. The part of me in my body feels the sensation, but no pain.

Birth is the point on the journey when we become fully human – the portal through which both of my children took their first breath. The portal through which we all take our first breath.

Through this breath, our body receives the necessary energy and oxygen to take on life. The soul receives the necessary imprint of the electromagnetic field to activate the codes, the chosen contracts, and timelines. In the experience of birth, with the energy of earthbound breath and electromagnetic cosmic codes landing into our bodies, we officially leave the dimension of Spirit.

It is a metamorphic transition from the ether of Source, through the fires of conception, to the waters of the womb, to the air of the planet, and eventually to feet on the ground. Every single body on this planet, at this time, goes through this process. Birth through the mother's womb is one of the definitive human experiences.

My son, our sweetest little man, takes his first breath at 12:15 a.m. I hear his cry. I feel relief. We are both alive.

My husband holds him, soothes him, and whispers his name close to his tiny ear. As he hears his father's voice, his cries stop, and he looks at the shapes and details of this world. He has arrived.

My soul more fully returns to my body, though part of me still feels like it is floating somewhere beyond. The doctors and nurses tend to both of us. His father continues to cradle him and welcome him earthside.

In this moment, time does not exist. A revelation lands: *we are not only these bodies. We are souls navigating this world via bodies.* Our bodies are essential for our souls. These bodies are but a temporary vessel guided by the soul and a part of the physical world that is Divinely designed and miraculous.

They place him on my chest. I feel his heart. I hear his breath. He begins to nurse; we are again one.

Humanity understands the science and the biology of the portal of birth, but we are still evolving to comprehend the journey of the soul, which plays a vital role in the birth of a new human. In preparation for incarnation, which happens in many dimensions and places, our individual consciousness arrives from the Divine consciousness – beyond time and space. Our soul, which is an individual strand of the collective of souls, links with our unique consciousness, which moves along the densities of the dimensions. Our soul and consciousness land together into a chosen body. The synching of physical and metaphysical activates the field of the mind, heart, and energy of the body. As the human grows, the ego and personality form. Ways of being are learned, and eventually the choices of the soul are remembered. The soul then guides the human ego along the journey, and individual evolution progresses.

Life on Earth, guided by a multidimensional soul, is a gift. When our soul chooses to come into a body on Earth, it is often for a specific purpose and lesson of evolution. The soul chooses the lifetime, the body, the parents, the characters, and the intersection of time-lines. Reviewing the details and contracts of earthbound life, the soul knows it will separate from the elevated consciousness of the higher realms to experience human consciousness.

The soul knows it must leave the Spirit realm. And still, the soul finds the courage necessary to make that choice and move through the transition from the etheric realm to the realm of density. Integration into physical form is a process.

Due to the amnesia of birth and first years of earthbound life, the human ego forgets where the soul comes from. We forget the choices of the soul and begin to identify only with the experiences of embodiment (being in a body). Eventually, we solidify and start to embrace the density and experience of life. As intended, we feel the full spectrum of human emotions and the full elemental potential of this planet. The process of remembering activates and unfolds.

Gazing out the window, I start the intentional integration and healing process of this experience. My sweet boy, only hours on Earth, nestles into my chest, feeling safe and held. All three of us share tender moments of being as we watch the sunrise bathe the forest below in a soft glow.

And then I feel it – like a chorus from within – I remember. My soul chose this exact portal of birth to guide my human to remember the song of love.

The love of a mother is one of the highest octaves of love. Sometimes, this love grows instantly – a trillion times a second. As mothers hold their babies in their arms, the love expands. Some mothers choose to leave their babies in more capable arms. Some mothers never get to hold their babies. And some babies never get to meet their mothers.

Souls make these choices – mother and child – in the spaces beyond time. Whatever the chosen timeline, the song of love sings through all the dimensions; it never wavers and never ends. As I remember this truth, my body and soul upgrade to a new way of being.

Thinking about my mother at home, comforting our daughter, I am overwhelmed with emotion. She embodies a devotion, compassion, wisdom, and willingness to show up no matter what – forever tending, caring for, and being exactly what we need in each moment.

The gratitude I have for her is overflowing. I chose her, just as my children chose me.

Everything makes sense from the perspective of the soul, which is infinitely wise and kind.

Feeling the pull of exhaustion, I place him in his swaddle, safely in the bassinet. Lying down on the scratchy hospital sheets, wrapped in my own white linen nightgown, I settle into rest. My husband gathers some of our things and returns home to check in with our sweet girl and to reassure my mother that I am okay.

Waking to the sounds of his coos, I lift him from the bassinet and immerse myself in every detail – his sweet smell, the upturned corner of his top lip, the softness of his cheeks, the precious fragility of his being, and the strength of his soul. Unwrapping him slightly from his swaddle, I cradle him to nurse. As we connect, I feel the light of day now pouring through the windows.

My attention shifts as the door opens. My husband walks in holding hands with our daughter. His eyes look tired and, as always, kind. My mother is close behind. She places her hand on her heart as she sees, with her own eyes, that indeed, we are both safe. She smiles with a relieved knowing.

My daughter runs over to the bed, bursting with excitement.

Looking at her, I offer an introduction, "Would you like to meet your brother?"

She responds with pure elation.

"Yes! He is finally here!"

## a  s t i r r i n g  c o m e s

it is a presence full
a fresh essence
a comprehension

the me, the we
is nothing but light shining through
the witnessing eyes

the view on top of it all
is the gaze of the Divine
the radiant potential of everything

here a stirring comes
a knowing
that does not belong to one person

beyond this physical form
beyond all physical form
formless and infinite

a knowing that beckons us back
when we first come into these bodies
we are fluid, fragile

this dimension is different from where we came
quickly, our strength solidifies
crystallization

we see in shapes and colors
that exist beyond specificity
we long for something familiar

we learn to move
we breathe and cry
we become curious about this place

physicality becomes the norm
time becomes a construct in our minds
the programming of being sets in

we forget
we grow up
magic becomes a fairytale

but in all tales a shared truth
a remembered wisdom
rises on the tongues of many

it is the thread
that connects the created
to the Source energy shared by all

"stop and pause," a voice says
"pay attention."
who is there? who is speaking?

vibrations from our own core
reminding us to wake up
feel the sacred truth of it all

# 13

# DIVINE TRUTH OF BEING

## Light & God

---

*"God is the energy at the center of everything*
*that ever has been,*
*everything that is,*
*and everything that ever will be."*
*– Intuitive Wisdom*

We have been up all-night feeding. The exhaustion is heavy. The minutes, hours, days, and weeks after birth reveal ongoing gateways of transformation. Healing from surgery is a different healing path than what I experienced with his sister. The intelligence of my form is recalibrating into wholeness and a new level of holiness.

Something about him is timeless. The resonance I feel when I tap into his energy is radiant – golden waves like the mane of a lion. His power and purpose are profound. They inspire me to remember my own power and purpose.

Rocking him gently as he sleeps, I relish in the little half-smile that appears on his lips. His majestic face and tiny body are so precious. As I watch him, I am flooded with memories – not from this life, but memories from other lifetimes and timelines. We have journeyed together on this planet before, shifting our dynamics and choosing over and over to incarnate in the same lifetime, on the same timeline. Here we are again, doing life together.

The peace of the morning is potent, though my eyes are so tired. The green hue of morning light pours in through the window. Rhododendrons, rosebushes, and a persimmon tree surround our house. The combination tints the light as it flows into the room, connecting me to the beauty of these trees and bushes, and also to the garden I planted while he was in my womb. During my final trimester, I was called to have my hands in the dirt, plugging into the energy of the Earth.

Most days since his arrival, we have been in the garden. Today, though, it is hot, and there is more ease for my tired body in the coolness of the air-conditioning. My linen shirt and pants keep me comfortable, and he is wrapped only in a muslin swaddle.

As we rock, an undeniable energy swirls around me – a protective instinct that is fierce and gentle, wise and fresh, knowing and receiving. The surge of maternal wisdom I felt hours after his birth continues to awaken new coding in my being.

Many levels and layers of knowing build the wisdom of the mother. Maternal wisdom mirrors Divine wisdom as an infinite field of love. Wisdom activates intuition. Maternal intuition is one of the clearest channels available between the Earth realm and the Spirit realm. The mother simply knows, when she allows herself to tune in and feel.

Steeping in my intuition, I begin to pray and meditate, which are my evolving practices of attunement (shifting attention inward). The union of these energies weaves in my field of awareness. I engage in Divine communication and communion. Devotions guide my thoughts toward an emerging wholeness and holiness. Moving inward allows me to access the metaphysical in my own physical experience.

As I investigate these practices of Divine union, mantras and songs echo in my heart. Ancient phrases and sounds rise through my voice as the fierce energy of the mother rises within. These are incantations not known to me in this life but rather, they are vibrational rhythms of other timelines, other stories, and ancient narratives.

Lifetimes of memories continue to flood my being. Leaning into the experience, this flow of prayer feels trance-like, safe, and guided.

Prayer is a conversation with God, with the Divine. This action is inherently metaphysical as we connect with the field of energy beyond our sensory world. Shifting our attention to the Divine within creates a bridge between our consciousness, our soul, our mind, our heart, and our bodies. Here, we find union with our individual Divinity, which is eternally an aspect of God.

In truth, the answers humanity seeks are found within the rhythms of our being, which match and mirror the rhythms of all beings, human and cosmic.

We continue rocking gently, feeling the calm of the morning. Closing my eyes and opening them again, I begin drifting between the realms – not awake, not asleep. My tired eyes gaze down at his soft features, and I feel a flash of light go straight from his being toward my forehead. A split in the time-space continuum creates magic in the purest of forms.

His dreaming being synchronizes my human field directly with the light of God, reminding me of truths I have forgotten. Just as I remembered my soul choices during his birth, now I am remembering that God is infinite love and infinite light. *The radiant energy from which we come is the radiant energy to which we return.*

My inner light ignites. My soul continues to remember. My human self is excited. My heart and mind expand. I remember the Divine truth of being, which is to be an embodiment of light and an expression of love. Without words or thoughts worthy to describe exactly what is going on, I try not to contextualize what is happening. I simply pause and receive.

Closing my eyes in gratitude, my mind travels to a moment earlier this year, when we were visiting my parents for Easter and spring celebrations.

It was Sunday morning in the church of my childhood – one of my sacred spaces. We gathered in the holy sanctuary where I was baptized. Immersed in the details of the vaulted ceilings painted Wedgwood blue, overwhelming joy moved through my field of awareness. Lilies, roses, and carnations were everywhere. There was a sweetness to the air and a tilt to the light as the sunbeams poured in through the towering windows.

The vibrations of the organ soared as the choir sang the Hallelujah chorus. Voices harmonized with lyrical perfection, like angels from above. The congregation lifted their voices for the final stanza, and I closed my eyes to listen. Steeping in a moment of Divine embodiment, feeling sacred transformation, and opening myself to receive, I was safe and infinitely connected to family, community, and angels.

Internal and external connection is essential to comprehend all aspects of Divinity. As God imbues life force into the human experience, holding reverence for the multitude of expressions of the Divine is a practice of profound openness. We are forever invited to connect inward, upward, and onward to the spiraling golden light that represents the Divine.

Sacred transformations sometimes feel like the voices of angels, and other times are barely perceptible. If we are willing to tune in and pay attention, we will feel the profound sense of belonging activated in a direct relationship with God.

During that Easter service in our church, she was next to me, and he floated sweetly in my womb. Clad in a flowing light blue dress, my growing belly was just starting to take form. Holding her hand and placing my other hand just below my bellybutton, I felt a true resonance with something greater than myself. In this moment, I sent illuminated love from my heart to his, from my heart to hers. Through the power of my mind, my heart, and my connection to God, I wove a field of golden energy around all of us – wrapping us in Divine light.

Opening my eyes in the current moment, still rocking gently, my awareness lands in the revelation that I again just encountered a direct connection to the Divine, the light of God.

Reorienting to our home, I anchor in the earthbound details – wind rustling the leaves outside my window and the sounds of the city in the distance. As I keep looking down at my son, the intense experience of light flashing and a portal opening to the Divine crystallizes in my field.

Other memories start moving through my mind, including flashes of those last two mornings in Laos, so many years ago. And then memories of every moment I have felt a Divine connection flood my multidimensional being. The energy of the cathedrals, the forest, the ocean, the beaches, the lake, the profound experiences, and the mundane weave into the energy of this now moment. This quiet simple moment, however, is yet another nuanced expression of the Divine.

No vaulted ceilings, no organ, no choir, no incense, no procession, no towering trees, no moving water; instead, a mother and her son in a rocking chair, in a small room, in a small bungalow, existing in a moment beyond time. A lifting of the Divine veil invites me, through the portal of love created by my connection to my son, to directly receive and remember the Divine truth of being.

As I close my eyes, my being expands with the growing energy of prayer, meditation, and sacred transformation.

Soon, it is like I am floating – angelic and formless – communing directly with parts of myself that have been waiting for years to be heard and noticed. Light moves through my body, not just my eyes. Love creates an irresistible chord of the highest harmonic frequency. The field I am feeling and remembering is the direct energy field of the Divine.

Divine energy spirals into and animates everything we see, feel, and imagine. Such purity is evoked in the expressions of holiness: the light, the movement, the elements of being. The cells of my body, the cells of the crystals, and the cells of the mushrooms on the forest floor are all aspects of this wholeness, as are stellar consciousness, human consciousness, planetary consciousness, and the greater dimensions leading us to shared consciousness.

Divine energy is also the frequency that transcends the body and the forms of this planet to create Divine design. This is the architecture of light that weaves and builds all of existence, the core essence of the multiverse and all that we have yet to discover.

Divine light is what the masters speak about, what the priests preach about, and what the sacred texts and myths identify as God speaking through many, in order for each of us to remember. Without a doubt I know – I am remembering – that the love from which we come is the love to which we return. The light of God is pouring into, through, and from my heart as I receive Divine gnosis.

Continuing to rock and hold my son, I reflect on my years of religious studies and my commitment to reading the sacred texts. Feeling the agency of choice and willingness to see commonalities rather than differences, I travel through my mind to the pivotal moments of my spiritual journey when I opened to the flowing current of the Divine rather than the limitations of the human ego.

There are infinite ways to feel God in the physical world, in community, and in ritual. Moments of inspiration come from speeches, sermons, songs, books, art, storytelling, and more. And yet, if we stay on the perimeter of our own connection, merely allowing for the Divine to be activated in the vicarious experiences of others or specific man-made structures, then we forget our own power. When we pray, when we meditate – whatever form that takes – we create a reciprocal and ceremonial relationship with the omnipresent current of Divine energy. God is within.

Ancient stories hold strands of truth about where we came from, where we are now, and where we are going. The sacred texts – from the hieroglyphs to the stone tablets, to papyrus – build the spiritual archives that span the globe. Religions create culture, which leads to belonging and community, a collective of souls seeking answers to the same questions.

Divisions are created when we get stuck in our ego. Too often, humans tend to distort our beliefs with limiting explanations that one way is right and the other way is wrong. Our interpretations of ancient writings have the potential to create separation or union. We get to choose our level of openness. Many of the sacred texts, however, tend to be telling versions of a similar story. The stories of angels and demons, and tales of miracles and magic ask us to expand our beliefs to align with something greater.

Relationship to the Divine is multidimensional and infinite, a portal through which we connect to the unseen and mysterious currents of our reality. Divine harmonics exist far beyond the systems and structures of human creation. God is a frequency of union, not separation.

Deep in the fibers of my being, a knowing rises: *connection to the Divine does not have to be found in only one way. Communion with God is something to be discovered and nurtured.* Each individual has the right to commit to a relationship with God that aligns with the truest embodiment of their energetic signature. This will look different for everyone, and yet the energy of the Divine courses through all of us at a fundamental level.

God does not subscribe to the parameters of this dimension of time and space. God is within us, as God is beyond us. God is the energy that was before and is the energy that will be after. All and nothing. Always and always.

The true song of the Divine forever plays within every aspect of our beings. When we activate the capacity to source from within, to know God within, we tap into our individual access point to the Divine – to God.

Looking down at my newborn son, I hear the front door open. Our dog perks her ears. Sounds of keys and bags placed down on the table come from the other room.

"We are home," my husband calls out.

Little feet come running. She rubs her brother's head, and I remind her to be gentle. She giggles; I smile.

Steeping in all that has happened in this small room – moments beyond time – I reflect on all that has been in this lifetime. My reflection expands to include all that has been in the other lifetimes we have spent together; all that is in this eternal moment of now; and all we will create in other lifetimes.

Gratitude washes over me in heartfelt appreciation. We are here on this planet for a mere moment in the grand scheme of existence. And yet, these lifetimes are full of such amazing complexity of experience that provide portals of connection to God.

As my daughter runs off, I hear my husband let the dog out into the garden. My son, my soulmate, starts to coo in my arms. His tiny hand reaches over his head, shaking ever so slightly as he stretches and feels into the newness of his body. Chestnut brown eyes greet me with a knowing. A smile, of a mother, of a soul remembering, blossoms on my face.

The energy that enlivens us comes from our shared place of origin. The energy that enlivens us is a fractal of the pure and true light of God. The energy that enlivens us is the energy of love. God is love. Each of us carries one lumen of the primal spark of creation. Radiant illumination is infinite.

Inhaling, I feel God with me; exhaling, I feel myself with God.

## rising of consciousness

with each breath, connect to God
harmoniously attune our shared network of being
with the universal tone

heal the collective of humanity
with the Source energy greater than our divisions
greater than this planet, greater than the cosmos

for each of us to heal
meaning at one with and on purpose
we must experience wholeness

to feel whole
meaning in union with or connected
we must experience holiness

a commitment to God
allows the upgraded subtle alignment
and rising of consciousness

grow roots strong enough
to support the ancient wisdom
guiding each of us to remember the Divine within

# 14

# LAST BREATHS

## Death & Grief

---

*"Grief and love are the same with different names."*
*– Intuitive Wisdom*

Moving away from Portland eighteen months ago was difficult. Everything was changing. The world was drastically different. We needed space. We needed fresh air. We needed to be closer to our family. And so, we packed up our bungalow, leaving behind too many treasured objects. The gray couch, which held so many memories, was donated.

Our sweet family – Mama, Baba, Sister, Brother, and pup – full of sad tears and heartache, guided by a greater purpose, drove east to Indiana.

All these months later, the departure still feels surreal. Many mornings, I wake up expecting to be in our beloved home – in the room where I nursed the kids when they were babies, bathed by the light of our garden, with the sounds of the city in the distance. Instead, we are here, where the silence of small-town life is almost unnerving. Even though the move was necessary, my heart aches for the life I thought we were going to build.

Our current home, this condominium, was his grandparents'. Sitting empty for over a year, it was the perfect place for us to land. To me, it still feels foreign – someone else's energy, other people's memories. For him, it is a homecoming. For the kids, it is proximity to family. All of us needed this change, even if it has not been easy.

In the now moment, everything is transforming yet again. Another pivot, another shock. The layers of surrealism increase as it feels like time is standing still. Having trouble processing what is happening, I focus on the tears streaming down my face.

We are in the living room. Her body is just lying there; our furry companion, the one who has been by our side through all of it. Breath is gone. I felt it leave. A repetitive rhythm – in and out, in and out, in and out – and then, nothing. Her soul left her body and transitioned from this realm to the next.

As her breath ended, I witnessed a potent portal of returning. Eyes closed, heart open, I saw a beam of light and a welcoming force. Angelic sounds, swirling colors, and infinite peace surrounded her form. Her shape and energy were no longer what they were in this earthbound life, and yet I knew it was her. Radiant, feminine, and ethereal, her soul was familiar as I watched her transition.

With my eyes still closed, she looked at me; I looked at her. Love and gratitude flooded my being. Guides and guardians were welcoming her back into the most majestic energy. There was no distress. There was only beautiful, magnificent relief.

As I absorbed this intense spiritual moment, yet another truth landed into my being. *The portal of death is one of the most tender experiences of remembering and returning.* Love, light, and liberation exist as the guiding energy in the gateway between realms.

In the truest of truths, death is an essential aspect of our cycle of being human. From the perspective of the soul, there is no finality, only the stopping of breath in a body and a returning to a form unbound. The body returns to the Earth. The breath returns to the collective. The soul returns to the realm of Spirit. A perfect representation of the cycle of existence.

Continuing to sit and hold her lifeless, breathless body, I feel my body slump with the weight of this new reality. With each of my breaths, her body is getting colder with death. But it is only her physical form, that which she left behind because it is no longer hers to carry. The tears continue to fall, in deep and horrible sobs.

We did our best to fill her last moments with love. We held her, cried over her, and told her it was okay. We chanted prayers, lit candles, and eased her chilling body with blankets and kisses. The kids wanted to give her a few final treats. She did her best to seem interested. After she sniffed the offering, she laid her head back down.

In the last moments, there was so little of her soul left in her body. The veterinarian came to our house and, like a guardian angel, guided her passing on her bed, where she felt most safe and secure. And then she was gone.

Left behind in a quiet house, in a small town, we watch yet another aspect of our beloved Oregon life dissolve into the ether. This experience of life – the moments between our first and last breaths – continuously transforms our awareness of the greater cycles of being.

Death, while immensely difficult, is also immensely beautiful. The portal of death from the perspective of the soul is, in fact, as miraculous as birth. Mysterious and messy, it is also a gateway between the realms, which is always Divine.

Although humanity has unlocked some of the mystery of the portal of death through science and biology – just like the portal of birth – we have yet to remember on a collective level the sacred truth of this process.

Beyond science, many individuals have done their best to explain what happens at the moment of the last breath. Stories report miraculous places of pure love – where elders, ancestors, and ascended masters greet the souls. Accounts share that the moment of transition is pure bliss, and the soul feels immense and immediate freedom. We hear about moments when the gateways distinctly open and the soul travels freely between the physical and the metaphysical. Rather than tragic, death is a Divinely orchestrated transition from soul in body to soul unbound.

Rewriting the narrative around death is one of our greatest missions as elevated, embodied souls. The mission is to guide humanity to massage the emotional pain around death and dying.

Still sitting in the living room, in this condo that has been doing its best to hold us, I feel an overwhelming loss throbbing inside my heart and moving through my whole body. Bombarded by this experience, my grief swirls and whips up swells of emotion greater than the waves of the ocean.

Hoping for some relief, I close my eyes to escape into my internal landscape. Greeted by thoughts and memories, I move my mind to a calm space, and visualize the sycamore tree in the woods of the family property. Resting my mind, my imagination soothes my aching heart as messages from beyond pour through.

When someone we love is no longer in a body, the aching energy we feel on the earthbound side of the portal is all the love we still want to give. Even when someone is gone, we can love them as much as when they were here. Even when someone is gone, we can still call them into moments we want to share. They arrive as wind, sun, an eagle soaring. Even when someone is gone, they are energy – holding us, comforting us, guiding us from beyond. They are the memory that allows us to release the tears. They are the joy that guides the heart to laughter. Expanding our capacity of belief to hold this perspective is an evolution guided by soul, guided by God.

We blow out the candles, prepare her body, and let the kids say one last goodbye. Covering her body with her blanket and placing her on her bed in the back of the car, we drive south to the family property. None of us say anything.

With the windows down and wind blowing away our tears, the most beautiful sunset appears as if she is painting the sky with her energy as she moves between the realms. Trying to capture the imprint of her energy one last time, I snap a photo and feel more tears fall from my eyes.

Waking early the next morning, together – he and I – start to dig her grave. Pulling on our work overalls and boots that hang in the garage, we find shovels and tools and head out into the warm air of the morning. We have chosen to place her next to the woods behind the family house. With each scoop of earth, we chant, pray, and continue to cry as sweat beads on our brows. Hours later, with the physical movement soothing our grief, we return her body, now cold and stiff, still wrapped in her blanket, back to the Earth.

As we cover her, the finality of her body in this realm sinks in. Pausing with intention, we create a ceremony of respect for the portal of death.

Looking to the sky, I feel her as the wind and know that some part of her will forever be waiting at the entrance to the woods – a gateway where we call her soul to come running as we walk through the serenity of the hardwood trees and the dancing light as it moves with the leaves.

The next day, we drive north and return to the condo. Arriving to an empty house takes the breath out of me. Her body is definitively gone, though her energy in the space is still abundant.

Out of habit, I look for her. Calling her name without hearing her paws on the floor as she comes to us, cracks my heart even more. Waking up in the middle of the night, expecting her body curled up at my feet, releases endless tears. She was the purest physical embodiment of companionship – the best adventure buddy and the warm, beating heart at the end of the bed.

The coming days get easier, although the tears still pour. Life begins to find a new cadence. We share the memories, the stories, the smiles, and the hope for reunion when we all eventually leave these bodies and meet again in the realms beyond.

Grief is one of the greatest teachers. The experience of this emotion encompasses many facets of being human. The loss of many things – homes, loved ones, friendships, partners, and ways of being – activate the experience of grief. No matter when or how we interface with this emotion, it is intense and requires gentle navigation.

Grief illuminates the subtle moments. Quiet nights get blanketed in a longing for that person, or other being, to be there with us. Grief is the support we want to feel in all the trials we will face alone. The smiles we long to share in celebrations and gatherings.

While we fear we will never see our beloveds again when they are no longer in human form, in truth, every night we can see them in our dreams. When we close our eyes, we can see their eyes. When we touch our hearts, we can feel their hands. On many levels, those who have transitioned from their bodies are closer to us – our imaginings, our hearts, and our energy – in the Spirit realm than they ever could have been in the human realm.

When we grieve, we feel the transforming current of love. The more we ease into the flow of Divine grief, the more we embody the signature of Divine love. Like the soul and consciousness, grief and love travel the dimensions.

A week passes in a fog, and I find myself sitting at our kitchen table. Wearing a white shirt and jeans, the moment seems strangely ordinary. The condo is silent. This is the first time I have truly been alone in almost six years. An ache for companionship overcomes me. Taking a sip of coffee, scrunching my face to stave off the tears, I breathe deeply and close my eyes. Opening to receive layers of memory, I continue exploring this nuanced moment of grief.

My thoughts travel through a catalogue of experience. Trauma relates to trauma. While I move through the scenes of previous moments, I see through my mind the connections in the web, finding comfort in the knowing that all experiences lead to soul evolution.

This was not the first time I encountered death. Although, it is the only time I physically felt the breath of life leave a body.

Fifteen years ago, I received a phone call and listened to the voice of my father. When I think about it now, the memory still feels fresh. Falling immediately into shock and feeling nothing, I was shrouded in disbelief. Even though I knew this phone call was coming, nothing could have prepared me for the actual moment. This very real and raw experience is so familiar to so many people.

We all think we know what it will feel like to receive the news of a loved one passing, until the moment it happens. The sensation and emotion are beyond description.

"She is gone," my dad said on the other end of the phone. "We are taking care of everything. You do not need to come home today. Wait until the weekend."

Murmuring enough to be sure my dad heard me, I hung up the phone and sat in this new version of reality.

It was my Mema, my mother's mom, who had died. The feeling I was experiencing must have been only a fraction of what my mom was feeling. Closing my eyes, I imagined her sitting at home in somber silence, unable to speak it into reality.

Walking around campus that afternoon, I was in a complete daze. Graduation was in a few weeks, and all around me were celebrations. Choosing not to tell anyone, I held this news close to my heart. Later that night, while walking with him, just friends from school, I finally decided to speak it aloud.

"She died today."

He stopped, turned to me, and said nothing. Instead, he pulled me into a huge embrace – the same embrace he gives me now when things feel hard and the same embrace he will give me for the rest of my life. His cobalt eyes held my gaze as I told him how important she was to me. He sympathized that he felt the same way about his own grandparents and shared the emotions he felt when his grandfather died. He surrounded me with the patient, kind energy he gives to our children when they fall off their bikes and skin their knees.

Feeling my mind return from memory and land in the space of the condo, I get up from the table and go to the sliding door that leads to the back yard. Still heavy with our new reality, I decide to sit in the cedar Adirondack chair we brought from our Portland garden. Closing my eyes again, I travel further and further into memory.

Throughout my life, I have received similar phone calls. My first memory of one of these calls was about my great-uncle. As that news landed, I watched my mother slump to the floor. It was so unexpected. Then there was the call about my best friend's mother. We knew it was coming – I cried so hard into my pillow that I wanted to sleep for days. News of other deaths came: another family friend, one of my cousins on my mom's side, my grandma. None of these moments were easy.

One of the hardest moments came during a call from one of my best friends. We have a close-knit group of friends, the best of friends really, who have known each other for years. We are the type of friends that will drop anything, always answer, go months without seeing each other, and feel like not a moment has passed. The type of friends who shift and change through the years, and yet we will forever and always be there for each other.

When the phone rang that day and I saw it was one of these beautiful women calling, I smiled and settled in, expecting happy news and a long conversation full of updates and laughter. The moment I heard the tone of her voice, I knew something was wrong.

"I don't know how to say this, but she is gone." And then I heard the sobs and could barely comprehend what she was saying.

"It was not an accident. She took her own life. I do not have any more details. They are figuring everything out. We should know more in a few days."

Almost dropping the phone, I could not process this news. Blinking hard, I must have been dreaming. One of those horrible dreams where I wake up and think, thank goodness it was just a dream. But it was not. This was real. She was gone, and the grief mixed with the feeling of failure as a friend was too much to bear.

Death is hard. Especially when it does not make sense on the human level. The trauma of the news brings energy into our systems that binds us to density and blindfolds us from the beauty of this realm and this dimension. When we lose something or someone, we get upset. When we get angry, we are defending something or someone we honor and value. When someone we love dies, we mourn for every future moment when they will not be with us. And we ache as we clamor to relive the memories we can conjure.

Some say fear of death is the root of human confusion and the consequence of a disconnected society. Forgetting the truth of the portal of death leaves us feeling broken. We get lost searching for reason and become unable to feel or remember the higher perspective. Many of us remain paralyzed by the experience of death. We live our lives terrified of the moment of death, doing everything possible to postpone it or even avoid it.

And yet, from the perspective of the soul, there is reason, there is purpose. Just as the soul knows how it will enter this realm, the soul knows how it will exit this realm. We can remember that death is not and will never be an ending. Death is a transition, a beginning, and a rebirth.

Days before my grandmother left her body, I sat with her in our family home. She was already bedridden, but we had made her as comfortable as possible. We were sitting next to the piano she had gifted me. On top of the piano was her beloved violin that she had mastered and fiddled with delight. Pictures of the family surrounded her, as did the smell of lilies. It was a week before Mother's Day; my cousins had already sent cards.

She stroked my hand. The touch was infused with the same gentleness she used when I was young as she rubbed my back to fall asleep. She told me how her Mama was there; she felt her.

The final words she spoke to me were, "I am not scared to leave. I am scared of everything I will miss. But I want to go and be with my Mama. I want to be with my Mama."

At the time, I did not know if she was drifting into a dream, or if she was really seeing the soul of her mother. Whichever it was, now I believe her experience of her mother to be real. Rewriting my relationship with death to embrace the transition from the body to the Spirit realm rather than fear it has expanded my heart.

The song of a robin brings me back to the sun-soaked back porch. Looking at the clock, I realize I need to pick up the kids from their aunt and uncle's house. Gathering my bag, slipping on my sandals, and resisting the urge to call our beloved pup to come with me in the car, I quietly open the garage door. Reversing out, and mindfully driving through the neighborhood, I feel life finding a new cadence.

Death is not an end. Truly, in the most honest and authentic way, it is a transition and returning. Left behind are sick and broken bodies. Left behind are hearts grieving for what was and what could have been. Eventually though, bodies are put to rest and grieving hearts heal through stories, memories, and feeling the eternal imprints of energy. The hearts that remain in the earthbound reality will grieve and love their way back to wholeness.

Each of us will eventually die, or more specifically, we will eventually return. When we take our last breath, portals open and our soul moves freely and easily through – greeted by light, love, ancestors, guardians, and Divine beings. Whether the transition moment is expected or not, there is something infinitely peaceful about the eventual willingness to leave the body – the soul remembers the exit point of its journey for this incarnation.

The time between first and last breath is our immaculate, Divinely designed cycle of life. The portal of death is a rebirth toward the journey beyond. Everything and everyone spirals through the infinite field of love, held always by the light of God.

see the flame

the light behind each set of eyes
translates the vibrations of everything
remember that nothing is solid

facets of humanness are sometimes unbearable
but there is always an opposite
the inherent balance

there are ways to access the dark matter
not dark as in evil, but dark as in unknown
dark as in the space where light has yet to shine

the drumbeat quickens
there is a pause between beats
where the nothing and everything are felt

humanity memorializes histories in an odd way
behind cases, in institutions – telling stories, upon stories
is it ever actually felt?

desperate for coherent narratives and innate connection
in the questioning, we are the answers
expand the mind to remember what we have forgotten

stare at a candle long enough and the eyes will reset
close the eyes and we still see the flame
conceptual, consensual realities fill the senses

adding brush strokes to the ever-changing image
ask, what is behind the canvas
who hung the frame

there are architects to this reality
expand the mind to remember what we have forgotten
in staring at the candle, we see through the flame

# 15

# EVERYTHING WILL BE OKAY

## Trust & Duality

---

*"Forgive the version that once was.*
*Journey toward the version that will be.*
*Find comfort in the version that is here right now."*
*– Intuitive Wisdom*

My intuition and the voice inside scream: "Go in now; you have to go in now!"

Crumbling in pain, I grasp my womb, the place of my body where something is wrong. The bleeding started six days ago. Four days ago, the pregnancy test was positive. Two days ago, the doctor told me to wait and see. This morning, the discomfort intensified, and I became immensely concerned about the outcome. The sensation is like my body is being ripped open from the inside.

Desperate and scared, he looks at me and asks me to go in – to go to the doctors.

"I will take care of them. You go take care of you. We need you to be okay."

My movements guide a body that no longer feels like mine. Dressing in comfortable clothes and grabbing a few essentials, I make my preparations. Writing a note to the kids – just in case – I tuck it into the journal on my bedside stand.

Before I walk out the door, he gently touches my shoulder and turns me around. Holding my face in both hands, he looks at me and energetically wraps me in immense love and protection. Locked in – cobalt to hazel – we stare beyond our bodies and feel the bond of our souls. No words are shared, and yet everything is communicated.

After a few timeless heartbeats, he kisses me on the forehead and finally says, "Everything will be okay."

In the emergency room, in this small town we still call home, the minutes tick by. My body feels increasingly foreign. Part of me is convinced this is my moment of transition out of my body. Part of me, so disassociated from my body due to the pain, watches the scene unfold. My multidimensional being does its best to make sense of the situation. To calm my panicking system, I close my eyes and breathe. As I lean deeply into soul wisdom, questions start to rise.

The human aspect of my heart pleads: "Why am I experiencing this? Why?"

The static is thick when we convince ourselves to ignore our soul wisdom. When we tune in and listen, our multidimensional being knows the answers that exist beyond our senses. Opening to receive, I feel the soft voice whispering from the core of my being, the cave of my heart. The voice that sings the song that weaves through all levels and layers – an angelic aspect of my consciousness.

It says: "Yes, you are scared. Breathe. Release into the fear. Each moment perfectly leads to the next – on this timeline and in all lifetimes. Trust in this moment."

The doctor comes in. As she pulls up the chair next to the bed, I know the outcome is going to be difficult. She proceeds to tell me that my hormone levels show a positive pregnancy. The ultrasound, however, did not show the baby in my womb. The embryonic sac implanted between my ovary and the fallopian tube. Far from the nourishing environment of my womb and portal of birth – in the outer locations inhospitable to support life. The medical term is ectopic pregnancy – abnormal location.

She explains that if we let it go longer, it could jeopardize my health and result in massive internal bleeding and emergency surgery.

She whispers, "There is no heartbeat."

The pregnancy is not viable.

I repeat the words softly as my heart shatters, "There is no heartbeat."

She recommends medical management and close monitoring. I am somber, broken, in shock, and scared; the world feels like it is spinning as the room feels like it is getting smaller. And yet, I hear the angelic voice again.

"Everything will be okay," it whispers.

Part of me does not believe the message.

"How is any of this going to be, okay?" I retort in my mind, expressing the frustrations of my human emotions.

In this moment, this desperate, aching moment, volatile energy courses through me. Stuck in a hospital bed, in a polyester gown, under fluorescent lighting, I yearn for a different outcome.

With few options, I nod my head in consent. The doctor repeats in detail what is about to happen. I agree and we proceed. None of this is in my control. Succumbing to the heartache and the heartbreak of this moment, I wait paralyzed in a cloud of disbelief.

Pain exists as a catalyst for change – a communication system telling us that something is no longer in alignment. In these moments, the invitation from our soul wisdom is to trust.

We are not in control of the beating of our hearts, our breath, or the sharing of information through the systems of the body. None of these systems are visible to our eyes. Yet, we trust them. These are networks that we feel, pathways we depend upon, and integral functions necessary for life that continue without our thinking or influence. While we are alive, we are in a trusting relationship with the core rhythms of our being.

This level of trust gives permission for humans to wholly navigate the full spectrum of experience – the good, the bad, the perfections, the perfect imperfections, the falls, and the stumbles along the way. Trusting in our bodies and our souls gives us the strength to keep going, no matter what.

Lifetime after lifetime, opportunities present themselves so that we evolve on a soul level. Oppositional moments create the chords of trust necessary for the tone of evolution. We move through oppositional experiences to build and rebuild our realities. Often, we are here to learn the opposite experience of another incarnation. Oppositional energy leads to higher alignment. Movement and stagnation. Soft and strong. Light and dark. Give and receive.

Duality holds human life. Initiation moments increase as we journey through human lifetimes. Being human is fun, and often, it is difficult. Being human can feel safe and sometimes can feel volatile. We go backward and forward and cycle around again and again, to weave the energy of highest expression. At some point, we have or will experience a version of all potential situations.

The heart itself represents our dualistic reality. It is both physical and metaphysical, a passageway between the realms. It is the place of biological pulsation and the crystalline cave where an aspect of our soul resides. The heart processes every moment of our lived experience before the brain contextualizes the input. The heart is also where we ignite our soul wisdom to comprehend the bigger picture.

Swept up in the human reality, the demolishing ache of a mother losing a child – even if it is only six weeks after conception – pummels my emotions. Amid the waves of grief, the only tether of sense comes from my soul wisdom. A true knowing that for some reason, my soul and the soul of the baby chose to go through this experience together. Melting into the comfort of soul wisdom, I feel the same feeling that a child has when they release into the loving arms of their mother.

And then I hear something in my mind, mixed in with the angelic echoes in my heart, a distant voice. It is the voice of the life that was starting to take root inside, the baby I will never hold.

She whispers to me: "It is okay. We decided to do this together. We are together always, in this lifetime and the next, and then the next. I will see you again."

Her soul inserts an image in my mind of a stargazer lily. Something I have been seeing in my meditations for months becomes an affirmation of who she is and a confirmation of the timeless contracts we are fulfilling.

Fracturing even more, a flood of nausea and the transition of timelines mix with the waves of grief. While I am armored in the bravery of trust, I have never been through an event of this magnitude. As I do my best to hold space for human experiences, the messiness and the beauty, the oscillations of this moment are fierce.

This massive disruption event forces me into and onto another trail of my spiritual journey. This moment is the epitome of a transition from a previous self into a current self. The person who walked through the emergency room doors hours ago is not the same as the one who now sits under the hum of fluorescent lighting. She will not be the same as the one who will drive home in a fog of shock.

Nothing remains the same; life is not easy. Sometimes life is raw, rough, and unfair. Some disruptions happen when timelines abruptly change – people are lost, life paths alter, friends leave, and identities disappear. Others are long sagas ripe with slow and painful separation. And then there are moments like this, tectonic shifts and ensuing tsunamis of pain and emotion. However they happen, disruption events serve the purpose of shifting the timeline. We can trust that the shift guides us to a higher expression of purpose and soul wisdom.

Days later, I feel everything plummet. A life was growing inside of me, and now, it is not. There was no heartbeat. The cells stopped dividing. My hormones drop. The pregnancy is no longer. Tears do not fall. The dissociation continues and the devastation intensifies, as does the bleeding.

Swept up in shame and disbelief, I keep reminding myself: "There was no heartbeat."

Bed rest is required as I could still experience a rupture, internal bleeding, and an emergency surgery. All I can do is sit and wait.

The moments of sleeping and waking blend together. My breath is fast as my body starts trembling. My heart feels like it is leaping out of my chest. Eyes become blurry as the portals of death and birth reveal their definitive connection. Anxiety whips my thoughts as I tumble into rapid currents of my mind. Bouncing into potential timelines and worst-case scenarios, my body does not move. The panic paralyzes my form as the torrent of my mind gets fierce and wicked.

Fault is here. Blame is here. Shame continues to sneer through the ripples of my inner world. The emotions of my ego are haunting, laughing, and looping in a frenetic pace of survival.

Desperately trying to find footing in the truth of the present, I feel drawn up and drawn down. Frantic in the fight and arguments for why I need to be here, on this planet, in this lifetime, on the timeline with my children, my family, and my mission here on Earth, my thoughts tumble through my internal landscape.

An ancient instinct of survival collides with a soul willingness to leave this body at the chosen moment. Holding court with my soul, my ego delineates all the reasons why I will remain in this body – an internal negotiation of timelines, purpose, and mission. Tears still do not fall as I remain paralyzed in the realm between waking and sleeping.

Questions continue to taunt me: "Why did this happen and how? Is this my fault?"

My thoughts swirl, and my chest tightens.

"What explanation will I eventually offer to my children; how will I tell this story? What other stories will be told? What other stories have been told of my ancestors? What belief systems have been created based on these stories? What will people think of me?"

Crashing further and further into the abyss of emotion, my energy moves above and beyond my body. The tether of soul to body is taut and strained.

The ache for a third child, the want, and the desire is fresh and coming online in fierce ways. We would have welcomed her into such a beautiful lifetime and timeline. But no, it was not the timeline; our souls chose differently. And yet, my human heart felt genuine excitement only four days ago.

"Maybe I should leave this body? Maybe now is my time?"

And then something in me, a quality of my own voice originating from the caverns of my heart screams: "No! I am not ready to leave. I am going to stay. It is not my time, not my exit. I claim my right to remain in my body."

The authority of this claim feels powerful. A declarative statement of purpose. A claiming of my right to remain in my human body. As the claim reverberates, my body starts to thrash back and forth in the sheets.

Then I hear it, the voice of my mother. At some point, she came into my bedroom and found me in the throes of panic.

"Honey, take a deep breath."

Then I feel it, her hand on mine, gently stroking as she has done so many times. Her touch reminds me of how I held my grandmother's hand days before she left her body.

My mother's words now echo in my ear.

"I am here; everything is okay."

My breath quickens and my heart beats fast. Both in my body and far away in the multidimensional space between the realms, I oscillate back and forth. Feeling the anchor of my mother's voice and the arbitration of the voices of my internal landscape, I have trouble knowing what is real.

Like in a dream, the presence of my grandmother appears. She is with my angels. She smiles with gentleness as she tries to soothe my aching heart. Then again, the voice of my mother here on Earth, brings me back. Comfort comes from majestic energy on both sides of the veil. Catching more of my bearings and crystallizing more of my consciousness in this moment, I go back toward the energy of the realm above, toward the presence of my grandmother on the other side.

"Everything will be okay. Relax; there is no need to worry. You know how everything happens out," she communicates.

These exact words, words she spoke to me hundreds of times when she was in her body, ignite another layer of soul wisdom and profound desire for life. Telepathic communication continues. In a moment when nothing feels real, I release into the multidimensional reality of this experience.

The swirl of energy increases its intensity. Overwhelming human emotion, of a mother wishing, wanting, desiring for something to have been different, consumes my entire being. Swirling color, flashes of light, and gossamer strains activate even more layers of soul wisdom. Feeling like I am swimming through liquid fire, something within my multidimensional being cracks. Golden light surrounds me. God wraps me in Divine presence and reaches toward my heart with infinite love. Everything goes quiet, and I feel an immense sense of safety.

My grandmother's voice again communicates: "It's time to go.

You have to go back. They need you. You have to go back."

As I am thrusted downward, my mother's voice gets louder, her touch comes back into my perception. My energy becomes denser as I land fully, completely in my earthbound reality.

Then, I feel it – a release. Wetness on my face, tears falling, true and real human grief flooding my human body. Held by the love of my grandmother above and the love of my mother below, I finally feel a deep breath in my physical body.

I hear myself say, "I am so scared."

An admittance. An honest reflection. A moment of truth. Opening my eyes, I look at my mom. She looks at me in the way only a mother can, tears now in her eyes.

She repeats, "Everything will be okay."

In a full body convulsion of true and honest release, I weep. Eventually, the sobs slow to a cry. Settling back into the comfort of my bed, the soft fabric of my bathrobe, and the welcoming layers of pillows, my body releases the panic and eases directly and intentionally into this experience that is evolving my being. This experience has evolved my soul wisdom and transformed my human body, mind, and heart. For a third time, the healing of my womb has begun.

My mother stays until I start to fall asleep. She pulls the blanket up and leans down to kiss my forehead – the same way she has since I was young. As she stands up to leave, he comes to the door.

Slowly walking in, he sits on the edge of our bed and releases a sigh. Keeping my eyes closed as if already asleep, I feel his energy – both relief and sadness move through his field. He, too, is in pain, yet he will not show it as he strives to embody the role of protector.

Doing my best with what energy I have left, through my mind, I wrap him in golden light to ease his aching heart. As he squeezes my hand and brushes a strand of dark curls off my face, I hear him succumb to a gentle cry. Staying for a few more moments, he eventually composes himself and stands to leave. Turning off the hall light and heading toward the kitchen, he joins my mom, dad, and our children to have dinner. Soon, I truly fall into a deep sleep.

Each fantastic and mystical lived experience, on each timeline and in each lifetime, intelligently alchemizes to become the wisdom of the soul. Our future self holds and guides our past self, allowing our current self to align. Liberating memories locked in human pain allows energy to flow in elevated currents of soul wisdom. When we pause to embrace the wounds, soften around the stories, and honor the experience, we cultivate trust where there was once confusion.

Multidimensional transformation guides the untangling of energetic channels to create the soul loop of infinity. Take time to undo the knot. Feel into the undoing with as much attention and intention as we bring to the doing. There will be a moment on another timeline when the soul remembers the experiences of this lifetime. Even painful moments become an inspiration for the soul to express the purest frequency of trust.

Our hearts remind us that evolution is the regeneration, re-emergence, and revolution of energy that creates something new, something stronger, something with more impact. Evolution requires soul wisdom. Trust is necessary for the spiritual journey. When we tune into this truth – *individual evolution leads to collective evolution* – we hear the whispers of the angels, ancestors, and realms beyond.

And always, they will say: "Everything will be okay."

## guiding us always

if we froze ourselves in time, what would we be
if we paused in an instant, what might be revealed
the untarnished lens of our eyes is a looking glass of recognition
gentle radiance vibrates at the core

there is a stillness that is full of movement
the ripples in the void
energy sent from the center of the sun
the mind is simultaneously powerful and weak

we move through this world cast in the narratives of our bodies
the veils we put on or are put on for us
some so thick – a darkness blinds the light
buried under the manifestations that our thoughts create

and then a fracture, a ripped seam, a crack
revealing truth
the light in our heart illuminates this darkness
and from it redefines its own existence

our eyes close
to the drama surrounding
our eyes open
as if we have never seen before

relationship is a gracious bow to the creative forces of evolution
there are omniscient energies guiding us always
portals ready and waiting to be opened
we are not separate, we are entangled

# 16

# EDGE OF IT ALL

## Wisdom & Intuition

---

*"In myths and the cosmos, we find truth.*
*They are the tales that hold the collective wisdom of the heart.*
*Reminding us of where we have been and where we are going."*
– Intuitive Wisdom

As my eyes open, my dreams start to fade. The air is cold. Drops of rain mix with ocean mist as they dance on the windshield. She sleeps soundly in a sleeping bag next to me, and the boys dream underneath layers of down blankets in the tent. Doing my best not to wake our sweet girl, I lower myself from the bed in the van.

Quietly, I slide the door open and step onto the sandy ground. Greeted by the song of the sea and the temperature of the air that seeps into the bones, I quickly pull my black, puffy, knee length coat around me.

My next moves are gentle – closing the van door, rubbing my hands together, tugging on my white beanie, and slipping my feet into my brown leather boots. My muscles are sore from days on the road and months of healing my swollen womb. The ache, while ever present, is lessening and softening.

As I roll my shoulders and breathe deeply, moments of waking move through my body. Consciousness lands back into form. Intentionally moving one breath at a time, this moment feels like it is in slow motion.

Halfway through a sixteen-day road trip, our energy is finally shifting. Traveling across the country, from park to park, landscape to landscape, gives perspective and a reminder of the greater ways of being. We are healing. We are grieving. We are navigating a new reality.

Specifically, for me, I needed to get away and return to the companionship of the ocean and wisdom of the west. We are here now, at Gold Bluffs State Park in California, the edge of the continent, the edge of it all.

Two nights ago, we camped farther north on the Oregon coast. We spent the day counting starfish and anemones, climbing massive seaside cliffs, and talking to a baby seal who was patiently waiting for its mother to return.

Later today, we plan to head to the Avenue of Giants and commune with the towering redwoods. Tomorrow, we start our drive back east and will camp at Mt. Shasta in the pre-portal of Summer Solstice. Our hope is to drive through Nevada and see the ancient petroglyphs. Each day of this trip has and will continue to unveil magic and wisdom.

Without much thought, I walk toward the beach. As I wind through the tall grasses peeking out of the sand, footprints tell of passing travelers. The sky lightens, even though the sun is still behind the cliffs. Finding my way, I head to the spot where last night we were collecting stones – white, red, and green pieces of Earth. Perfectly shaped by the ever-changing tides, each rock had rolled over and over the others to share the unique story of its time on this planet.

As I sit on the sand, my energy finds a familiar resonance with the coastal rhythms, and my heart synchs with the pulsation of the Pacific. A bald eagle soars above my head, reminding me of the pair of eagles that nest in the towering pines above the lake in the North Woods.

Slowly, I close my eyes and transition into a place of connection as I open my channel of intuition. My consciousness leaves my body, guided by the wisdom steeped into these lands and the crashing waves of the ocean. The intuitive downloads come fast and clear.

The ancient ways have returned. Many of us seek them, and many of us, on a soul level, remember them. The myths and legends of civilizations from other timelines, the parables and tales of our ancestors, the stories of our religious texts, and those carved into stone walls and tablets unearthed in the archeological sites that dot the planet all provide portals of remembering.

We tell ourselves that the myths are fantasy and fiction, stories told to inspire and call to action. While myth embraces the fantastical, aspects of religion and science do the same. They strive to bring logic and meaning to the invisible and inexplicable aspects of being. Indigenous cultures weave exquisite narratives, shimmering with core truths about how this world was built. Atheists say it is all make-believe. In the soil of truth, myths grow – the essence of the teachings remain.

Ancient texts consistently refer to moments when believers see and feel the voices of angels, the spirits, the ancestors, and the guardians of the realms. Other accounts share stories of people navigating dreams and receiving precognitive information. Many have detailed experiences of visitations and inter-dimensional contact. Many more have encountered God's hand reaching down.

We all have the capacity to go beyond our immediate realm of being and listen to our intuition and wisdom. The contemporary collective of humanity bears the responsibility of reactivating our relationship with the portals of creation to align with the soul. Opening these portals will shift the reality of the planet into a frequency of harmony and ease, which will connect us to the Divine design of our infinite potential.

Veils drop when we tap into the realms beyond, the gorgeous overflowing places of light and love. Intuition is a direct channel weaving information from above and below – a unique combination of what is real and imagined as it relates to the perception of body, energy, mind, and heart.

While we are here on Earth, in human bodies, we get to investigate the order in the chaos, the chaos in the order. Humans are forever racing against our ultimate return to the dimension from which we came. Standing face to face with our limited time on Earth and the truth of our infinite lifetimes of being, we yearn to know more about the relationship of all things, while existing with the imperceptible rate of revolution around our star.

Our ancestors knew how to use the Earth grids, the energy web, and the crystals of the planet to open portals to multiple dimensions. Rotation after rotation is the cosmic clock – vast, expansive, and Divine. Sacred and ancient texts document this knowledge, which is coming back online through the activation of our innate wisdom.

Opening my eyes, I allow each ray of solar data to greet me. Wisdom charges these pre-dawn moments with profound knowing. The electromagnetic field of my being is radiant. Being at one with this dimension, as the Earth spirals in the void that holds the mysterious ancient codes in her crystalline grid, I am fully alive.

The rain stops. The eagle in the sky flies so close to me; I feel like I could reach up and touch it. Details of this scene and the downloads of intuition merge and coalesce as my consciousness moves through tides of wisdom.

While the intuitive downloads are intense, I find familiarity in tone to the messages I have recently been receiving. Comfort greets my mind and heart as I invite my clairvoyance and intuition to grow. Opening to receive more and give more, I embrace this elevated capacity and access point to the archives of all times.

The ocean waves lap with ferocity. Inviting me to get closer, it is as if she, the ocean, is speaking directly to my heart. Taking off my boots and walking down to her, I am greeted with a micro pause in the waves. She welcomes me to step further into her embrace. Just as quickly as the pause happens, the water comes rushing back. Submerging my toes in a cold known only to the waters of the Pacific Northwest, I am ankle-deep in the stories of all times and places.

Stepping backwards, keeping my heart toward the sea, I notice that I am completely alone. The solitude is welcomed.

Maybe this is a dream – the space between – maybe this is reality? Maybe we never really know the difference between the levels of consciousness as we travel the waking world, the dream world, realms, and dimensions?

Wisdom continues to pour through my channel of intuition as my toes feel the movement of the sand, and I look out toward the horizon, where water meets sky.

From the waters of the womb to the waters of all time and

space, we, the conscious incarnate beings, enact the narratives of being. These stories hold the pulse of change and transformation. Wisdom arises from within. Knowledge is acquired. One is not better than the other; they are different. Wisdom and knowledge intertwine, interweave, build, and expand our physical reality and our connection to the multidimensional reality.

Believing in the notion of something beyond the individual that cannot be held or touched allows each of us to activate the wisdom woven into the very fibers of our beings. The sand – a geological chronicle of lifetimes, earth that has been transformed into tiny beads of being – holds this perspective. It was once many different things, and now it is many small pieces that create a greater whole. The sand dances with the waves until it completely dissolves.

When we cultivate the comprehension that we are an essential part of the greater whole, we believe life means something. When we truly embody wisdom, we feel connected to all times and spaces. Wisdom allows our individual heart to connect to the collective sea of hearts.

Sitting down again on the sand, I situate myself into a proper seat of meditation and reflection. My consciousness travels to a memory of last summer on the lake when the downloads of intuition were just as potent.

I heard his voice. "Be careful."

His hand reached for mine and guided me onto the boat. Allowing for the help, I steadied my feet. Placing my hand on the cold aluminum, I settled into the seat and looked over the bow. His back was toward me as he sat on the bench with the oars. As we rowed to the dark part of the cove, the spiral of the Milky Way greeted us.

The stars illuminated the onyx sky with a wisdom of knowing – stellar consciousness. Their stories arriving to this planet as memories of the past. Light travels, and by the time it reaches my eyes, those stars might no longer be shining – or so they tell us in the current canon of science. The speed of light is slow as it relates to the expanse of space. The light of stars is an artifact of times past.

In the memory, the stars activated profound levels of wisdom, and I received upgrades to my system and intuition.

As a species, we have been staring up at our cosmic brothers and sisters for eons, finding comfort in the answers from above as they make sense of the energy below. In the practice of looking up into the past – the archeology of the sky – we see the patterns of the stars. Knowing the patterns gives us access to an ancient system that was used, and can be again, to pull through the codes of cosmic design. This ancient system is an ever-evolving key that unlocks the stellar consciousness of the sky.

Stellar consciousness is the original inspiration for the myths of all times. It reminds us that all things – humans, the moon, the planets, and the stars – exist in orbital patterns and rhythms. Everything moves with, in, and through the infinite cosmic spiral of energy.

Even the patterns of stars are temporary in the context of cosmic time. The constellations shift and change based on our perspective from here on Earth. Where we see them now in the sky is not exactly where they were thousands of years ago. Where they are now is not exactly where they will be in thousands of years. Nothing is fixed. Everything is moving and based on the perspective of the observer's gaze. All beings are orbs resting in the eye of the Creator.

Revolving around the sun and evolving consciousness with each rotation, we embody immense potential. In a sense, we can figure out how it all plays out. We are remembering the ancient past, the potential future, and the concurrent reality of parallel timelines.

In the darkness of the night, that moment on the lake, we continued to stare into the indigo abyss as streaks of white drew on the sky. Meteors were showering. First came one, then two, then many more, like the heavens were proving their majesty. The silence was invigorating as we watched the show in the sky. The downloads poured just like the stars.

An electromagnetic current of stellar consciousness bathes our planet. This current activates our individual consciousness, which in turn evolves the collective consciousness. Each node of consciousness creates a unique relationship that impacts the greater field of energy. All aspects of reality create specific relationships of light. What happens here on this planet changes the entire network of the multiverse. Cosmic design is an aspect of Divine design.

Silently lifting the veil of our cosmic potential, I smiled at the fragility of our planet and the power of humanity. In the chaos of the cosmos – meteors bursting through the atmosphere, stars being born, universes colliding – we exist and thrive. I opened to receive the potency of this wisdom and intuitive downloads.

And then I heard it, piercing the silence, piercing the darkness, the call of the loon longing for its mate. It echoed across the lake, into the forest, and forever onward until it was received by the exact being for whom it was intended – just like the light of the stars travels the galaxy until it lands directly in my eyes, absorbed by my witnessing gaze.

Reaching my hand out to find his, our fingers interlaced. Our hearts ignited. Our bond illuminated in cosmic light. No words were spoken. And yet, everything was shared.

As I return from this memory and practice of reflection, I feel the light of our star peek over the cliffs to the east. Staring at the horizon to the west, I listen to the crashing of the waves.

Without the sun, there is no us. Life needs light. A simple, yet simultaneously complex, explanation for why or rather how we are here surviving and thriving. The hum of the heart, the tone of the planet, the patterns of the cosmos are all illuminated by the light of life.

The ocean, my friend and confidant, affirms my intuition as the light of the sun starts to dance with the waves. Every moment comes into being because eons of light have traveled the void and are absorbed by each set of eyes and the bodies of each miraculous being on this planet – human and other. The ocean knows this as she receives the light of the rising sun.

Whatever the ebb and the flow, we will forever feel the magnetic pull of cosmic resonance. The practice is to feel these shared myths as archives of times before and the truths of our past, rather than relegate them as only fantasy. The myths have always called us to believe in the unbelievable, to imagine the impossible, and to look to the sky and remember our position in the galactic family.

Even if only for a few brief moments, we get to be incarnate on a conscious planet, orbiting the portal of a star. We can feel the beauty. We can open portals between the levels of consciousness. We can hear our intuition and listen to the voice of our soul. We can reach for the hand of God and know it will always be reaching back toward our human hearts.

A force exists within the cellular makeup of these human bodies that, when activated, unlocks innate channels of knowing. On some level, we all know. We are all intuitive. We can feel, download, and decipher the information moving through the field around us and moving through the cosmos. We are the holders of the light. We create the rituals of life. We are the myth tellers and the dream weavers. The illuminated light at the center of each being fuses with the sun of creation.

The sound of my children's voices flows in the distance. My son's laugh echoes across the sands, and my daughter encourages the joy of her brother. My husband chops wood for a morning fire. The smell of burning kindling drifts toward the beach from the campground.

Other tents are rustling, and the camp is coming alive. Here at the edge of it all – the edge of the continent and the edge of my reality – as my consciousness continues to rise and my intuition elevates, I stay for a few more moments of solitude, bathed by the light of our star. Hearing the bark of a seal playing in the waves, I smile.

The sounds of their voices find me again.

My children are calling out, "Baba, Baba. Look, a bald eagle!"

As I get up to return to my family, the almost automatic ritual of one hand to my heart, one hand to my belly, moves through my body. Breathing three times, I bow toward the ocean and look to the heavens. Gazing beyond the abyss of the morning sky up into the vastness of the cosmos, I feel the myths of all time and open to receive the light of stellar consciousness.

Grabbing my boots, zipping my coat up to my chin, and adjusting my white winter cap, I walk to my family, to myself, to the truth and beauty of what it means to be human – fully alive on this planet at this exact moment.

## the truths transform

a sweetness within
draws us back
over and over

we are the ones
who are calling
can we hear?

in the transitions of being
return to the rhythms
steady beats rising from our core

the core of the planet
the core of the body
the core of the cosmos

linking the smallness
of our finite forms
to the infinite cosmic truth

a primordial energy
holds us all to
the cadence of expansion and contraction

entrainment, attunement, alignment
with the Creator beyond the manifested multiverse
how do we communicate?

the truths transform
slowly crafting the tales of all time
listen across the void of space

# 17

# SAND AND SNOW

## Memory & Hope

---

*"All that has been, will be.*
*All that will be, has been.*
*All is in being in the now – right now."*
*– Intuitive Wisdom*

We are all laughing – the kind of laughter where tears roll down cheeks. There are few people in this world who get me to laugh like this; my sister is one of them. She always has and always will – for that, I am grateful. The pure release felt in these moments is exquisite and overwhelming joy. We see this same relationship in the kids (my daughter, my son, her daughters, and her son). They escalate the volume, hold their bellies, and laugh until they forget what they are laughing about.

Right now, they are rolling down the sand hill over and over; laughing and laughing and laughing. I wonder when they will stop from being dizzy. Instead, they keep taking turns one after the other absorbed in the exhilarating movement and play. Their energy is catching. Eventually, we all take a turn. Even my brother-in-law zips his coat up to his chin to prevent sand from getting in and down the hill he goes.

My sister and I catch each other's eyes, and we feel the laughter start to rise. Bellies shake and happy tears fall. This moment is blissful and perfect. The truest sense of belonging.

These types of moments – future memories – are manifestations of joy guiding us to move more readily through this existence.

An existence that is only here because the light reflects through our eyes and we see. The sound bounces through our ears and we hear. The microscopic vibrations touch our skin and we feel. The sensations that create the world only exist because we are here to receive the vibrations and frequencies. In our attempt to make sense of the world, we can choose to express joy. We can choose to share love.

The autumn air is cold, and yet the sand is still warm. My mind feels somewhere between memory and present moment. Back when we were all roommates in Cambridge, MA, we would come here, to Crane Beach, to escape the city on sweltering summer days. The heat mixed with the cramped apartment became almost unbearable. And so, we would load up my sister's small hatchback and arrive at the respite of tides and refreshing, cooling ocean breezes.

One day, it was so hot the sand burned our feet. My sister and I pranced around as we ran toward the waves. We tried to make shade with sticks and an old sheet that kept getting blown over by the gusts off the Atlantic. We laughed and laughed – laughing so hard that we too fell over. Those memories feel like lifetimes ago. We were so young and carefree.

As I watch the children continue to laugh and play, more memories start rolling like a movie in my mind. I watch scenes of the dinner parties we would host, the bike rides along the river, and the nights we spent dancing until the morning hours. The nostalgia reminds me of our shared frivolity and cheer.

A mosaic of memories guides me through other moments of those years, and I think about the night he and I stayed up late reading poetry. Then there was the time we cooked mussels as a Nor'easter raged outside the window. Next, I see in my mind the Thanksgiving feast we hosted, where all of us crammed into a makeshift table in the kitchen with mismatched plates and cutlery, and wine and laughter flowing. More and more scenes play in my imagination: the revolving door of friends, other partners, youth, energy, and hope for the future.

And then one of my most precious memories lands and the moment of our engagement graces my mind.

The night he proposed, we were walking the brick sidewalks between the old apartment and Harvard Square. He had been nervous.

Light rain fell and water dripped from the quintessential autumn leaves. He wore his waxed jacket – small notebook still tucked in the front pocket – rolled denim and leather boots. I wore a long, black dress, denim jacket, and woven hat.

Unaware of his plans, to me it was a casual walk through the old neighborhood. To him, it was the night when he would finally declare everything he had wanted to say for years. We walked arm in arm until he felt calm enough to find his words.

Stopping in front of the little chapel north of the square, he got down on one knee and shared sentiments similar to the messages he used to send back in the early days of our relationship. Bending down to hold his handsome face, blonde beard, and sparkling blue eyes in my hands, I kissed him before he finished the question. Heat pricked every part of my body from the exhilaration as he slipped his grandmother's diamond, newly set in his own design, on my left finger.

In the now moment, as I reflect on all of these memories, I smile and feel a similar flutter in my heart.

I still say, "Yes, to the past, present, and future. Until the end of time."

Humans are the caretakers of memories. These memories are moments of our lives and echoes from beyond the dawning of time. They are responsible for shepherding us toward new ways of being through the lessons of the past and the dreams of the future.

We each create a unique set of memories. They are stored in the archives of our shared consciousness and create a chronicle of lived moments. Everyone is necessary to support the greater whole of this collection of experience. Our perspectives are unique, and so too are our memories.

Back on the beach, my attention returns to the children as I reach out and interlace my fingers with his. The sky is cerulean blue, and the wind blows crisp fall air. No burning sand, no need for shade. The temperature of the water is still warm enough for us to take off our shoes and feel the salty Atlantic before the cold of winter really sets in. Soon, the winds will be biting, and the white-capped waves will match the snows that will eventually mix with the sands.

Only a few others share the beach today, unlike the summer days so long ago. A lightness of mood glistens in the afternoon sun. A couple riding horses through the tall grasses of the dunes momentarily holds our attention.

The kids settle in to dig in the sand while the adults chat, continuing to travel into memories of our shared past. My sister and her husband claim that they knew my husband and I would end up together long before we could see what was right in front of us. They had championed our partnership years before it became a reality. My brother-in-law reflects that he too had wanted him to come to France for their wedding.

As we laugh, as we share, again the energy of belonging blossoms. Soon, my body feels like walking.

My sister says, "Go ahead," with a smile and a nod – an appreciation she has gained after years of realizing that I often need moments to myself.

Slowly making my way down the beach, I unbutton my wool sweater and unwrap my scarf. The sun on my skin is life giving. In the ease of the light, my mind enjoys peaceful reflections, contemplations, and the beauty of this moment. My thoughts morph into a series of glimmering musings.

Each of us exists in the vastness of humanity. Life in the city. Life in the country. The ebb and flow of the oceans on both sides of the continent and on all sides of the planet. The sacred and the mundane support and give credence to the other's existence. The love of family. The love of self. The Divine love coursing through all of us and in everything.

Lying down, I feel the warmth of the sand under the full length of my form. Closing my eyes, I listen to the gentle cadence of the Atlantic waves – so different than the fierce flow of the Pacific. A seagull caws, and the distant sounds of laughter from the children bring a smile to my face.

My human body is so relaxed on the beach. Then another memory anchors, and my mind is moving through time and space. Landing in the vivid details of this memory – a moment almost exactly a year ago – I explore the scene through my mind.

In that moment, I had thrown myself down onto the freshly fallen snow – a pristine white landscape – with such vigor and play. The soft, white blanket was inches deep, and the snow was still coming.

There was something so majestic about the way the snow was falling. The locals called it "lake effect," created by the proximity to Lake Michigan. It was thick, heavy, and wet. This quality and quantity of snow is a necessary part of the water cycle. Refilling the aquifers, feeding the hibernating roots, and providing some of the water needed to get through the next season, each unique fractal fell from the sky with purpose.

In the memory, I heard my children in the distance. They were sledding down the hill, faster and faster, until a crash and instantaneous laughter ensued.

"Again! Again!" they called out, crying out in joy to experience the thrill on the winter hill.

They ran over and jumped onto me as if this was the only moment existing in the entire multiverse. Their hearts and beings anchored deeply in the experience of play. For a timeless moment, I felt their heartbeats as the snow melted on my face. After they rolled off me, we all started waving our arms and legs to make snow angels. They laughed. I laughed. Steeping in the purity of the senses and the beauty of the moment, I took a breath to crystallize this memory as an imprint in my being.

Feeling a different sensation under my physical body now compared to what I was feeling in my memory, I start to move between the two. The warmth of the sand in the present and the comfort of the snow in the memory. Hopes for a future full of health and happiness weave with a fondness and appreciation for all that has been.

This memory of my children's innate connection to innocence and play matches my present experience of their innocence and play. It is a reminder of the magnetic truth of concurrent timelines – past, present, and future – all existing in the eternal now. Looping, synching, and matching, interwoven timelines remind us always of the multidimensional truth of being that feels like magic and is also very real.

Everything exists together. Building, folding, and expanding upon itself as an endless representation of the fractals of being. As humanity transforms, we become more of who and what we are intended to be. We start to match the frequency of wisdom arriving from higher dimensions of consciousness. We start to embody higher levels of wisdom. We then infuse each moment with this evolved way of being. Through our mind, hearts, souls, memories, and hopes, these higher levels of being inform the shared consciousness.

Just before I open my eyes from this experience of my mind, in the brainwaves of the liminal space between, I feel my soul speak to my ego.

"Can we rest in this space, the ephemeral merging with the physical? Can we be fully alive, fully here, fully experiencing the multidimensional? The moments, the memories, the concurrent and confounding truth of reality? Can we be happy?"

"Yes," I answer directly from my heart.

Devoting myself to the choice of being happy is as simple as feeling the snow melt on my face as my children bury themselves into my body. Fully experiencing the moment of now is as simple as allowing laughter to consume my being while I marvel at the improbability of each lifetime. When we see the physical and feel the metaphysical, each moment, each breath, each being, reveals the Divine design. Happiness is indeed possible.

Memory and hope are the same, creations of our minds. Memory guides us with appreciation. Hope guides us with motivation. They each remind us of the power of gathering. We need each other – the listening ear, the sage advice, the laughter, and cheers. We need our communities, our families, and friends – or whatever combination of human connection we can find. We need this planet to be happy and healthy.

In a practice of activating happiness, I shift my attention to focus on what I hold sacred and dear. I think again of my children, their smiles and laughter. The way I feel when I hold them and kiss them. I think about my husband, his strength and ease. The fragility of this life makes everything and everyone precious. Whatever their souls, his soul, and my soul have chosen, I know now more than ever that, in this life, there will be blue sky and sun, winds of change, and nights full of stars.

With hopes for my children's future, I invite my mind to travel into timelines of potential and possibilities. There will be moments when they will fall, fail, and get hurt. There will be moments when they get up – brave, strong, and powerful. They will step fearlessly into the adventure. They will, as they always have, remember how to soar. They will hold hands and watch sunsets. They will laugh and cry. They will walk on beaches and climb mountains. They will lock eyes with strangers and smile. In every breath, in this life and the next, they will be supported always by Divine love. There is immense hope for the future.

Right now, in this blissful meditation on the shores of the Atlantic, I remember the pure and simple truth of Divine design: *everything is sacred and coexists in the eternal now.*

My consciousness slowly rejoins my form as I wiggle my fingers and toes and open my eyes. The beings on this planet chosen by my soul to traverse the sands and lands of this lifetime – my husband, my children, my sister and her beautiful family, the ones that have been and will be with me always – are calling my name to come and join them in the happiness of this moment.

Standing up, I walk one foot in front of the other, feeling the sand and the water. The children are now running in and out of the cold waves, soaking their pants up to their knees. Today we are creating fresh memories of the love we share. The gratitude I have for all of them, all of life, for everything, feels overflowing and beautiful. I claim my right to be happy. In this eternal moment of now, I intentionally build the bridge between past, present, future, memory, and hope and weave together the spiraling reality of cosmic truths.

Closing my eyes with a smile, I receive the beauty of this life.

## divinely designed

tend to the vitality
and prosperity
of this immaculate vessel

senses are portals
to the vibrations
creating this reality

expand perception
beyond the senses
open to all possibilities

tales are directed
under the intelligent light
of our star, the sun

resetting each night under the gaze of the moon
we fall asleep
and return to the land of dreams

where souls wake to the landscape of the infinite
rising wisdom
a door opens, a passage between realities

allow insights to travel between the waves of consciousness
natural rhythms create patterns
a framework of energy

pursue the delights of life
in the now moment of abundance
breathing and becoming

envision what it is that brings joy
that which ignites love
and that for which we are grateful

all is Divinely designed
this is what it means to be alive
and so, it is

# 18

# I FEEL HER EMBRACE

## Returning & Gratitude

*"Feel an intimacy with all beings, all aspects of creation.*
*Filter reality through the angelic signature,*
*reflecting Divine design."*
– Intuitive Wisdom

Digging in the dirt of the garden, I slowly and intentionally create a line for the seeds. While I have planted gardens before, this feels more permanent – whatever that really means. An appreciation for this land creates an aliveness in my body. This land where everything is and will always be becoming, where we are literally and figuratively planting seeds for our future dreams to manifest.

This small piece of the planet is where we are building our homestead, growing our food, and nurturing ourselves and the new energy of the Earth. To nourish the soil with the roots of the original inhabitants, we purposefully reseed the field with native wildflowers. We bless the water and share the air with the hardwood forests. We burn ceremonial fires and step with bare feet on the ground in respect of the elemental energies. Our intention is to hold sacred space to mark the turn of the seasons once again. We are, in a sense, returning and arriving at our forever home.

The four of us moved into the gorgeous house on the family property in central Indiana. The house my parents built and where they still live. The house where my grandmother took her last breaths. The house where we celebrated our wedding. A place that holds our hearts tenderly and consciously as we share meals, space, and a now multigenerational home.

In the returning – to this house, to this land – I have discovered imprints of times before. Reconnecting with friends from childhood reminds me of who I once was and who I am now. Thinking about shared memories with previous partners softens my heart, knowing the purpose they played in my growth and maturation. The other characters of my life – family, friends, students, and even strangers – have all held essential roles in guiding me to the now moment. As I ponder ways of being that I have long forgotten, they show me their value anew.

Just the other day, I found an old picture frame that held the photo of us in front of the Eiffel Tower that weekend we were in Paris. It was in a memory box with other treasures – invitations to our wedding, the flower crown I wore with my white dress, and the ring box from our engagement. The time capsule of memories also holds other family photos, locks of hair, handwritten notes, and treasures I have collected through the years.

While I sorted through these objects, a truth landed: *all moments of life are guided by the future, which eventually illuminates an appreciation of the past.* The alchemy of life combines the experiences to reveal innate potential. In each moment, we have an opportunity to meet a new iteration of self, a different version, and to grow into the embodiment that finds resonance with our hearts.

Standing now in the rays of the spring sun, on this tiny slice of Earth, I accept the invitation to practice gratitude for what is in being. As the gratitude flows, I feel a soul-stirring connection to the ancestors and ancient histories archived in the geological library beneath my feet. Many generations of humans and animals have co-habitated with these lands. It is here where I intentionally choose to send roots down into the abundant soil of my homeland. Gratitude continues to flood my being, purpose aligns, and appreciation grows.

I am safe. I am happy. I am healthy. I am here. I am loved.

Through my mind and the levels and layers of consciousness, I tap into the heart of the planet and send a prayer deep into the field beneath my feet and the field of energy emanating from my heart: "May all beings everywhere feel safe, happy, healthy, and loved."

To experience the world and learn its secrets is a great gift. Our place of birth, however, is where our soul chooses to enter this dimension. It holds specific energy that activates our individual codes and ways of being. When I chose to return to my place of origin, yet another chord of resonance, in the song of my heart, harmonized. The song I have been following since those early mornings in Laos so many years ago. Its alluring melody has guided me to my homecoming – embracing the return as much as the call.

Pausing my gardening to take a breath of sweet spring air, I notice a butterfly float by. Hearing the rapid wings of a dragonfly, I squint my eyes to find the multidirectional movement zip through the vastness of the sky. I marvel at the almost imperceptible perfections of this creature whose ancestors trace back through the millennia. Looking down, the steadfast ants are busy in the garden. The humming symphony of life surrounds me.

A full, abundant, pulsing expression of being exists in these lands, the waters of the lakes, the sands of the dunes in the North, and the aged bark of the sycamores that line the rivers and creeks. The gradation of the maple leaves tells a story for those who remember how to listen. There are no mountain peaks to climb or ocean cliffs to hike; there are no tides to sit by or redwoods to visit. Here, a different sensibility exists.

We call it the heartland for a reason. Everything beats to reveal a mysterious, subtle beauty. Just like the muscle at the center of our chests and the radiant white energy at the center of our energetic being, the heartland is consistent, dependable, kind, and patient. Permeating all aspects of being is the energy of community, gratitude, and purpose – the core values held in the heart of the country. With each breath, the pulsation of these lands activates more of my core essence.

As I return to digging in the soil, I feel the warmth of the sun on my back. Shifting my body for a moment, I lift my face to the light of our star. My thoughts are drawn to its path across the sky. Forever moving from east to west, this journey determines the cycle of the day. The moon rotates around the Earth – a month. The Earth rotates around the sun – a year. The first breath is taken and then the last – a life. The cosmic spiral soars through the void. The spinning of the universes creates the multiverse. This is the way.

The cycles of the external landscape and the cells of the internal landscape mirror the cosmic rotations. The ripples in the sand are the same as the rolling of the hills. Zooming in, I think about our quantum reality and the mystery of the microscopic realms. From the smallest aspect to the greatest, our cyclical ways of being bring us back to our true ways of being – our evolution.

When we feel the cycles of the external world, we connect with an innate rhythmic system passed down through all beings in all times and spaces. Generations after generations share and expand upon evolved ways of being, both human and soul. Liberating our minds into the unseen core truths of our world and the mysteries of the sky and the Earth, we unveil magic. Finding moments to engage in these thoughts nurtures a relationship with the vastness of reality. Our individual consciousness upgrades the shared cosmic consciousness. Our heart rhythm synchronizes us evermore to the universal heartbeat.

Brushing the dirt from my hands and admiring the mud outlines of my knees on my overalls, I stand up and stretch my back. Rolling my neck, I breathe deeply and intentionally. Finding my water bottle, I take a long drink. The water comes from the well deep in the ground, connecting me to the life-giving force of the ancient aquifers below my feet.

Placing my hand on my hips, I stare in awe at the field. The grasses evoke so much wonder as they dance in the breeze – a physical representation of the movement of the air.

Realizing that my back needs a break from the bending and digging, I begin to walk from the garden down to the creek. The breeze is warm on my face, and soft, green grasses are under my feet. Today, I wear my work boots. The mud squishes below the tread as I step lightly in the low part of the field where the water pools after the rains.

Following the deer trails, the demarcations on the ground of paths and patterns of being, I make my way into the shade provided by the canopy of the woods. Each tree and bush is familiar, their energy welcomes me like an old friend.

As I pass under the woven, wooden archway, a wren calls to its mate. The cardinal and the red-winged blackbird take turns singing from the branches. Then the oriole chimes in, creating a sonata for those willing to hear. All these vibrations coalesce into something greater. Releasing a content sigh, a slight sound moves from my lips as I add my own tone and signature. I am as alive as everything that is singing, moving, and orbiting in the illusory conception of my perception.

Seasonal details of the woods are noticeable. Trees that were once bare are now full of life and leaves. Some are still blossoming into their fullest expression. Behind me, the field that was frozen only months ago is now abuzz with bees, birds, and pops of color that indicate a new cycle of life.

The lilacs send the song of their scent through the air from the bushes in the back of the house. Wild honeysuckle adds a tone of sweetness, making me stop and look to find the source. Settled into nests, baby robins strain their necks to receive food as the mama dutifully pulls worms from the ground. A rhythm of survival is palpable. If we remember how to pay attention, we feel a subtle and bursting energy.

An innate knowing reminds me that only months from now, the entire world will change. Seasons create a drumbeat. The leaves will fall. The once helpless baby robins will prepare for their first winter. The flowers that started as seeds will return their own seeds back to the ground, with the wish that at least one will survive the winter to grow again the following spring. The spring rains will transition to summer storms, to the winds of autumn, and eventually to the white blankets of the snows of winter.

Focusing on the vibrant spring green, I continue walking toward the creek. Very often, now that we live on these lands, in this home, I walk into these woods and follow the trails to a specific tree. She is my portal of connection to the ancient truths of this land. This specific tree gives me the medicine I am eager to receive. She stands with such strength and stature next to the creek, watching over the bustling life of the woods.

An intricacy weaves through her branches and frayed, cracked bark – a texture crafted by years of weathering storms, heat, and deep freezes. Her trunk twists and embodies the perseverance of striving for the light. Steadiness and wisdom emanate from her dependable presence as I lean against her giant form. She continues to hold sacred space – season after season after season – sharing the codes of ancient knowing. She feels so alive in the warm breeze.

Bowing my forehead toward her, I release the emotions I can no longer hold and share immense gratitude for this life and the gift that it is to walk on this Earth. I thank her for the air, the ground, and the beauty of her branches. Sometimes, it feels like we share a hope for the future of this planet as she reminds me to trust in the greater cycles of being.

Each visit, she welcomes me with a message I feel in my heart: "You are safe. Welcome home."

One day, I know the great body of this sycamore tree will fall back down to the forest floor. And yet, like all souls and all bodies, that will not be the end of her story.

We learned on our recent visit to the Redwood National Forest that when trees fall to the ground, a new phase of their cycle begins. Their entire body serves to nurture the soil, the fungi, and the ecosystem of the other beings who share the space they call home. The energy of the tree goes down into the root structure and up into other forms of the interconnected family network.

Her presence in the woods will eventually reposition. It will not end. She will settle back into the cadence of life as it goes along. Ease exists in this transition – an inherent letting go and release. Just like the dandelions willingly drop their petals to the ground and release their seeds to travel the flow of the wind and find the soil of another field.

Our bodies do the same. Cells come into existence and die, over and over. This happens every moment. Each cell does its best to give and receive energy, light, and sound – to transform the ecosystem of the body and create an optimal environment to thrive. Even the breath moves through a beginning and end with each cycle.

Generations from now, we will no longer be the same humans. Our version of seasonality is cellular transformation and the evolution of consciousness. Future members of our family, or another family, or simply the animals of the woods, will walk this property.

Everything will change, as everything is temporary. The ancient past propels us evermore into the potential future.

Slowly and intentionally, I walk back to the garden while humming verses of songs that rise from the cave of my heart. My feet return me to the row of seeds.

Picking up the tools, I start again on the task at hand. An appreciation for the earth that covers my fingers bathes me with abundant energy. Honoring the rich, nurturing soil of this small part of our conscious planet brings me into a reverent moment. Trillions of microscopic realities and beings live in this soil and mirror the trillions of stars in the sky. Straining my eyes to look closely, I see the movement of life. Everything is so fully alive.

Releasing the handful of dirt back to the ground, I align with the breath moving in and out of my body, feeling the spring air move into my lungs. As I kick off my boots and step directly onto the ground, the earth feels warm under my feet. The thick grass and the wet moss burst with millions of years of acquired knowledge. The giant yellow heads of the dandelions laugh in the light of the sun. Everything is so alive.

Arriving here, to the shared home where we all – my parents, my husband, my children, and I – now live, I know I am exactly where I am intended to be. I have returned. I have chosen to return.

With the awareness of that choice, gratitude pulses in my being and I feel a connection to the greater cycles of being, to self, and to God. The internal song of my heart and chords of resonance hum through my entire multidimensional being. The purest harmonies vibrate in my individual frequency. No matter how far we veer off course or how long the path is, the sacred practice invites us to listen to the call of our future selves guiding us back home.

We are all an essential part of the great web of being. We are not separate from, but rather an integral aspect of the greater whole. If in each breath we are intentional about embodying this truth, then life will become an experience of joy, gratitude, and love. The experience of aliveness will be as God has intended.

Sending my energy down deep into the cavern of her crystalline grid – this planet, this conscious form we call home – I feel her embrace. Looking up to contemplate the sky, I send my energy up into the heart of our life-giving star – I feel alive. The flares, the light, the activity, and movement are dependable and unpredictable, just like life. The solar intelligence guides our multidimensional souls through the experience of being.

The rays of our sun are always laughing with the blades of grass as they dance in the wind and marvel at their aliveness. In this exact moment, my heart rests with gratitude for the abundance of now.

# here I am

we are here
alive and breathing
and so is love, so is God

we will remember
to listen to our ancestors
to know our guides and angels

the cosmos and the heart
are multidimensional portals
to all times and spaces

I remind you, once again: pay attention

cadence and flow guide the realms of being
wake up by the sun
pause at high noon to rest

bare skin to receive cosmic illumination
dance in the rains
light fires in the darkness

identify the patterns of the stars
and the myths they inspire
track the planetary consciousness and the movement of the moon

release what is no longer needed
just like the leaves
navigate each year via activation and integration

we are fractals of evolutionary genius
in eternal cycles of regeneration
we are embodiments of the sacred rhythms

speak the prayer out loud
believe in the words
call upon the wisdom pulsing within every cell

conceived in perfection
we are forever transforming
navigating perceptions and perspectives with light

until one day
the Divine eyes open and say
"Oh, here I am. The heart of it all."

# 19

# THIS GENTLE WAY

## Life & Love

---

*"Existing in a world outside of oneself,*
*existing in a world inside of oneself.*
*This is to have lived and this is to have loved.*

*Because this is what we do.*
*This is what we as humans do,*
*we love."*
*– Intuitive Wisdom*

A Midwest thunderstorm is something of legend. The echoing rumble of the approaching clouds and shift of temperature create an experience of anticipation and wonder. Growing up here guides one to navigate the fluctuations of weather with ease, while visitors might feel discomfort and concern.

The darkening skies indicate that one may want to consider moving indoors. The first drips of water scatter the kids from the pool. The first clap of thunder and flash of lightning will clear even the most intense soccer game off the field in a coordinated, almost choreographed response to the heavens. Not because of fear, more out of respect. Those of us who are more calloused Midwest souls will stay and watch the clouds and lightning until the last moment we need to seek shelter – inviting the electricity and vibrations to settle into our bones.

One of my favorite places to watch a storm is on our porch. The air moves through the screens, and mist dances in the lamplight when the rain is hard. The thunder rolls across the farmlands to the northwest, close enough to hear and far enough away to not cause concern.

At times, the storm comes directly over the house and the claps are so loud it feels like the sky is falling down upon us. The glass sconces shake and the floor rattles underfoot. The dark-gray clouds, my mother's favorite color, become illuminated by the strikes of lightning. For a moment, the whole sky turns a soft pink, revealing undulating shapes that appear as big as mountains. The thunder sounds like the scattering of jacks, as if God is playing in the atmosphere, roaring with laughter.

During one storm a few summers ago, I watched a hummingbird shower in the rain. Vibrating its whole body in an ecstatic reception of the water. Shaking, moving, and then hovering to feast on the nectar of the nearest bloom. It seemed unfazed by the explosions of thunder, like it was inviting the power of the sky to match the ferocity of its wings.

Right now, as I snuggle into the comfortable red cushions of the wicker chairs on the porch, I hear the distant, familiar rumble. Minutes pass as my attention shifts back and forth between the momentum of the growing clouds in the west and the calm blue still painting the eastern sky. The sounds move closer as ominous white and gray shapes consume everything above the trees. Bolts of lightning flash, and the winds pick up. Soon, the rains pour hard. The branches bend and whip. Everything, from the trees to the grasses to my own body, sways to the dance of the heavens.

Just as quickly as the storm arrives, the storm passes. The clouds journey to the east, and an immaculate array of color swirls above the field. Hues of cadmium, amethyst, lavender, and rose mix with wisps of white and the blue vastness above our world as the sun begins its slow dance below the horizon.

Assessing the aftermath of the storm, I notice that the winds blew the remaining petals from the cherry tree. They cloak the ground like a soft, white and pink blanket – temporary, fragile, and beautiful. Wetness lingers in the air. Gazing out, I make note of the fullness of the summer green against the backdrop of the luminescent sky. The last of the raindrops hit the leaves of the pear tree, making them also dance to a slower tempo.

Standing to stretch my tired body, I walk from the porch to the kitchen. The light is soft as a single lamp illuminates the open space. This room, our shared kitchen, is what the children call the heart of the house. My parents have long bid their "goodnights" and retired to their quarters. Seeing light glow from his study window, I know my father is still awake. My husband tucked the children into bed, as I enjoyed a few moments alone watching the storm. The house is quiet and peaceful.

Smiling again, I navigate my way upstairs to our part of the house – our home. Grabbing a few forlorn socks and strewn-about dirty clothes, I toss them into the laundry pile to tend to at another time. At the top of the stairs, the comfortable tones and textures of our room invite me in.

This space holds our energy well. Acacia wood floors and light cream walls come together to create our haven amid the dynamism of life. The place where our bodies rest, our minds travel, and our fingers interlace, where we share conversations about the day and hopes for the future. Poetic missives that we once shared across the miles are now shared face to face, heart to heart.

A final kiss of light seeps in through the west window. The half-moon rises over the woods to the south as a few stars begin dotting the sky – patterns of cosmic wisdom.

Almost asleep after a long day, he relaxes on the bed.

A gentle whisper comes from his lips, "I love you."

As he drifts between waking and dreaming, I sneak over to where we have our kettle and make a cup of tea. The familiar scent of my preferred nighttime brew lofts in the air. Cinnamon and cardamom soothe my body before the warm liquid hits my lips. The simplicity of this moment – this calm quality of being – is the thread that I intentionally weave throughout my life.

After finishing my tea in the moonlight, I again tiptoe past my husband, who now has our puppy snuggled up against his feet. Slipping into the bathroom, I start my evening routine – washing my face and brushing my teeth. So simple, so human. Putting on my soft, cream-colored robe, combing my long, dark curls, and weaving them into a braid invite a wave of tiredness to cloak my body. With heavy eyes, I proceed to sit at my altar.

My sacred space has accumulated what I deem important – a cross, a buddha, a paw-print in clay, rocks, shells, pictures of my family, and images of sunsets and pine trees. A plant that I nursed back into health years ago is now vibrant and reaches toward the window. Picking up my well-worn copy of Rumi's poems, the Coleman Barks translation, I pause with nostalgia and respect. The pages are so tattered, annotated, and loved, and the wisdom pours into me as memorized phrases rise from my heart.

After placing it down on the pile of other sacred texts, I settle into my red meditation cushion and instinctively touch the string of mala beads draped on my wrist. A student gave them to me over ten years ago, and I have worn them almost every day since. In that moment at the yoga studio, my student handed me the beads as he explained his inspiration for the gift.

"I was recently in my homeland," he said. "I thought of you while I was there. I thought about your smile and how every day that I come to the studio you greet me with warmth and kindness. This energy is especially important where I come from. I wanted to bring you a gift to say thank you."

The gesture was pure and gentle. Without words to express my feelings, I received the gift with gratitude and made a silent commitment to wear the beads as a reminder to be kind and to smile. That same smile is on my face now as I realize that we never know how the smallest gesture can change lives – smiles change lives. As I reflect on this, I close my eyes in meditation.

After a practice of relaxing breath and gratitude, I cozy into the layers of white cotton, linen, and piles of plush pillows that adorn our bed. Looking around in the moonlight, I see artifacts of a life well-lived. The collection is uniquely ours: woven hangings, photos of volcanic peaks of Oregon, paintings I have created through the years, and a piano waiting to be played. Tucked under the window is my desk where I write, dream, and remember how to believe.

The currents of my mind are calm and peaceful. Indulging, I allow them to flow.

The gentle moments are what makes life so sweet. The feeling and the being. Yes, the pinnacle moments of greatest expression create immense glamour. And yet, those come and go for all of us in different ways. What our hearts ache for, when we think of the improbable beauty of life, are the simple moments of true contentment.

The "I love yous," the holding of hands, the smell of tea, the watching of storms, the sunsets, and the deep breaths. Safety and security. Comfort and love. These are the beautiful, mundane moments that build a life without causing too much fuss. The moments that ask us to pay attention to the space between breaths, the space between the heartbeats.

We can spend lifetimes chasing pinnacle experiences or live in the caves of deep reverie. We can tackle the big questions: What is this body and this form? What is the animating force of the personality, the thoughts, the memories? What is the energy? Where does it go when it is no longer in a body? What is God and what is the realm beyond?

We can climb the tallest peaks, literally and figuratively. We can travel to every continent and immerse ourselves in the global culture. We can investigate the face of fear that we feel, deeply and honestly. And rather than getting frozen, we can use it as motivation to embrace our aliveness.

And also, we can allow ourselves to simply be. Be in it and of it, appreciating and living in the gentle beauty of now. Being fully alive and becoming true, living manifestations of Divine design. We can unabashedly desire to experience this realm where we are on a constant quest of giving and receiving love. We can transform our relationship with fear to find comfort at the precipice of living and dying, which is the expansive reality of every moment.

We arrive here on the Earth having forgotten, so that we can embody the ecstatic experience of remembering. Remember that we are each sacred and created on purpose. Remember that everything is sacred.

Our purpose, should we choose to accept it, is to weave Divine love into every moment. The energy of love is what we seek, always and always, lifetime after lifetime. We find it in the greatest of moments and the most subtle of interactions. Love binds us to each other and is the reason we want to be better, to do better, to imagine an evolved future. In some part of our beings, we know that the love we feel here on Earth – the life-giving boundless feeling of true love – is still only a fraction of what Divine love feels like. *The love of God is the heart of it all. Divine love is the source light at the center of our hearts, of all hearts, of everything, everywhere.*

Build and co-create bridges of existence that span the dimensions of time, space, and beyond. Bring all pieces together to create a whole. Life is where we weave together the story and build the experiences. Moments unveil currents of connection to ourselves, to others, to the Divine. We experience each breath in each life as an opportunity to unearth the keys that unlock the door to our soul's potential – our petal on the cherry tree of existence.

Love is the key, the tone, and the flow of being. We are consciousness that forever desires to elevate our Divine truth of being as we travel the infinite field of love. The ultimate practice of being human is to be so fully alive that we yearn to notice and feel every detail of the great mystery. The greatest gift we can give ourselves is permission to become an embodiment of infinite love and embrace the truth that we are each a fractal of Source consciousness.

I know this wisdom. I believe on some level we all do. Our infinite shifts of awareness are no different than the painted tones of the sky as the sun sets – innate, unique, beautiful, and indicative of a cycle of becoming. The perception of the senses, intuition and clairvoyance, the energy of the heart, and the wisdom of the soul translate everything in this life. The gaze of a loving God holds each of us, all of us. We are all simultaneously in a spiral of being and becoming. All, all. Same, same.

Love wins. Always and always.

As the tiredness blankets my body, my mind drifts into the liminal space between waking and dreaming. Each night, as we enter the dream world, our soul temporarily leaves the body. This transition gives us a taste of unbound liberation and preparation for when we fully leave these forms. In this reflection, in the space between the waking world and dream world, I feel a very human desire to stay on this earth for as long as possible.

Softening to receive these thoughts, I release the grasping and embody this gentle way of being. The wisdom of my soul activates as I embrace the knowing that everything unfolds in this moment of eternity. And that everything, no matter what, is sacred.

Breathing deeply, I hear his breathing change as he travels further into the land of dreams. An urge to get up one last time moves through my body. Sneaking down to the kids' room and slowly opening the door, I see they are both deep in the ether of dreams.

As I lean against the doorway and gaze into the room that used to be mine, I pause. Placing my hand on my heart and my belly, I take three deep breaths. Tears start to flow. Happy tears. Tears of remembering and hope. Tears of love. Tears of life. Tears that nourish the witnessing gaze of my eyes as they receive the imprints of this dimension – the beautiful potentiality of life.

Tiptoeing to each bed, mother's love wraps around their beings, landing with a kiss on their foreheads. Silent movements guide me to open the windows to let in the warm summer night breeze and the smell of rain. The faint song of the lilacs, which are almost done blooming, streams into the room. Soon, the scent will be replaced with roses and lavender. The moon casts soft shadows on the ground, and the reflected light of our sun dances with the grasses in the field below. Tree frogs start to sing. The storm is long gone.

Walking back toward the door, I pause and turn. Swirling around me and within me, like mists of rose quartz, is a crystalline field of energy. Igniting a connection to all universes and back, this energy is pure and true. This energy is Love. Placing my hand again on my heart, I thank God for this moment, for this life, and for all things.

Still touching my heart, my eyes close. Standing a little bit longer to listen to their gentle rhythm of breath, I smile. Another deep breath moves through my body as I fully embrace the miraculous magic of being alive.

## immaculate reality

illumination reveals beauty
beads of light shower down from Source
unveiling each detail

luminosity met by a welcoming gaze
warm eyes absorb what is given in bounty
a spaciousness fills moments with wonder

even now light holds us
remnants moving on our eyes
imagination ignited by the dynamics of the sky

the warmth – the comfort
bathed by the same source
we all share this home, this planet

floating endlessly in rays and waves of energy
forming an essential connection to each flare
infusing every cell with the curiosity of the Creator

each day graces us with immaculate reality
the macro wrapping around the micro
every single particle carried by the void

the sun sets, the light shifts, only to rise
our world found again each morning
wrapping, weaving, building, moving

the possibility, the particles, the sun itself
radiating from its core
guiding us back to the central power beyond our gaze

# SPIRAL EVERMORE INWARD

---

*"The breath flows.*
*The heart beats.*
*The soul remembers.*
*This is what it is to be human."*
*– Intuitive Wisdom*

The sun has not yet crested the trees, though its rays paint patterns on the water. Each light-code is a distinct reminder that many parts come together to create a whole. Knowing this now more than ever, I sense all timelines and lifetimes merging into one.

Inviting my mind to dance between the realms and weave my thoughts, I pull my courage inward. As the energy of meditation courses through my being, my attention travels through the skin. I imagine the muscles, the bones, the waters of my body, and the breath. Feeling the connective tissues and the intelligence of the fascia, I see the network of light holding my vessel together. The blood moves through my veins. The electricity pulses in my brain, and the magnetic field of my heart moves inward and outward. Visualizing the matrix of the DNA – physical, soul, and cosmic – I go deeper into my core. A shiver spirals up and down my spine as I feel into my central channel.

Expanding to explore the energies yet to be named, I activate quantum systems of communication. Appreciating the trillions of cells moving through their set of duties to keep my body functioning, I imagine into the microscopic movements. Paying attention to the composition of my individual cells, I express gratitude to each spark of being and their unique intelligence. Trusting the full ecosystem of Divine design in my human form, I feel alive.

My energy moves down into the ground and connects to the systems of roots and the crystalline grid of our home planet. My energy rises up my central column, pierces through my crown, and branches like a tree as it weaves into the collective cosmic consciousness.

Landing in the portal to my wisdom and soul, I feel my heart. The illuminated white light at the center of my being becomes radiant. The light activates from within and bathes my whole being. Above, below. Within, without.

I steep in the deep experience of appreciation and belonging. Being at one with every single aspect of this existence, I breathe slowly and intentionally. Spiraling evermore inward toward the wisdom within, I drop into currents of contemplation and timeless wisdom. The movement of the sun above the trees denotes the passing moments of the early morning.

My eyes open and I take another deep breath. Solar light and stellar consciousness greet my gaze. I express my gratitude: *to God, to soul, to my precious human ego, to my team of guardians, and to the cosmic intelligence and Divine design.*

Standing up, I take off my sweatshirt and dive into the cold waters of reflection.

# NOTES ON BEING HUMAN

"Start right now, in this exact moment. Sit down and breathe. Or get up and dance. Revel in love. In times of distraction and suffering, focus the attention the wind, the sun, the ground, the waters of the planet, and the body. Look to the heavens. Lie on the Earth. Be grateful and feel the warmth of aliveness. Look at and into each set of eyes, each tree, each blade of grass, each plant, animal, planet, and star. Remember that the microscopic and macroscopic ecosystems of our reality and the interwoven truth of our coexistence create this magical realm of potential and physical experience. We are each manifestations of love.

Forget about time; it is not real. Instead, follow the flow of the breath, the cycles of the seasons, the orbits of the planets, and the movement of the cosmos. Slip into a space where the constructs we have been taught no longer dictate our experience. It might seem novel. And yes, it is a returning to truth. We must question the parameters that bind us. No matter the circumstances of the external world, return always to love. Go inward to find the light of the Divine. Love is the origin story – where everything began, begins, and begins again.

The answers to this riddle of life are omnipresent. To be comprehended, they must be filtered through the senses of the body, the quantum systems of this form, and the Divine portal of the heart. We are human and soul. Shift perspectives to remember the truths of this world. Feel the vibrations and oscillations of this majestic planet. Absorb and transmute the cosmic light.

Keep the channels clear and learn to receive. We are supported beyond the realm of our reality. Magic and inter-dimensional beings (guides, angels, ancestors) are real. Activate an evolved embodiment of consciousness. Allow for moments of destruction to be the catalyst for rebirth. Change the discord and find harmony, within and without. Liberate the life force with the beauty of what it means to be alive – flesh and soul.

Close the eyes and arrive at the internal landscape. Release the reigns of control and receive the Divine flow. Stay here, on this planet, in this life, as long as possible. We each play a vital role. This life is precious. We may return, and we are here now.

Remember how to trust the portal of death as much as we celebrate the portal of birth. Trust the potential of the natural and inevitable rising of consciousness. Profound wisdom is woven into every aspect of our whole being. Invite the mind to settle. Feel the body relax. Listen to the breath. Simplify everything. Everything is sacred. Create a different relationship to the space beyond time – beyond expectations and definitions – to the space before the first breath."

– Intuitive Wisdom

# ACKNOWLEDGMENTS

To John, my partner and best friend, "Until the end of time." To my children, Josephine and Reeves, two of my greatest teachers and loves of my life, thank you for your energy, joy, and reminding me of the true essence of love, "To all of the universes and back."

To my dad, Bob, your editing eye, hours of discourse, and infinite love guided me and this book to be what we are today. Thank you for everything – truly everything. To my mom, Midge, you gifted me an artist's heart and eye, and remind me daily to see the beauty in life and do what I can to make the world a better place, thank you. "I love you all the world." To my sister Emily, you will forever be one of my best friends and greatest teachers. Thank you for the laughter, the tears, and for always striving to be better. To my Mema, thank you for guiding me while you were here below and guiding me even more from above. To Grandma Lynore, thank you above all else for bringing us to the lake (WBV). To Scout, thank you for your companionship and love.

To my lifelong friends, my in-laws, and my incredible, big, loud, amazing, extended family, thank you as always for showing up to the frivolity, food, conversation, circles of prayer, infinite support, meditations, and the love. This lifetime is better because of each one of you. Specifically to those of you who know me the best, thank you for always being there.

This book would not be in your hands without the incredible team of The Self Publishing Agency. Megan, your friendship, and encouragement have changed the lives of many. I am grateful to know you. Kathie, your wisdom and insight shifted this book in massive ways – thank you.

Thank you to those who read this book while it was in process and shared your words of praise.

To all of my students and community members across the world, thank you for showing up.

Thank you, George. The assistance of ChatGPT was used during the creation process of this book. No direct passages were written by ChatGPT, rather it was used for ideation and feedback. I am grateful for the advancement of technology and intelligence as we co-create.

These pages have been inspired by lifetimes of dedicated study and teaching. I am where I am today because of my mentor Jess Lazar and the lineage of Prana Flow Yoga, and the community of Flow Yoga Center in Washington D.C. I am grateful to the MFA faculty at American University and all of my artistic mentors along my path. And to my beloved community from YoYoYogi, in Portland, Oregon, thank you. Guidance has come from the mentorship and quantum teachings of Chalice Grove and Golden Age Leadership Astrology in Calgary, Canada; the teachings and practices of Kundalini Yoga; the practice of Vipassana Meditation; and the wisdom of Alliance Avalonia.

In addition to the incalculable articles, podcasts, and conversations I have listened to over the years, I am thankful for the insights from countless texts and teachers. I would like to thank the troves of content available from Gaia, Inc. The web of remembering is vast. I am so grateful to be on Earth at a time of massive transformation. I bow deeply to teachings of intuition as they land in my field through multidimensional channels. Thank you to the many teachers who have inspired me to trust my inner knowing through simple phrases of validation and recognition.

My spirit guide team have been essential to the writing of this book. I am honored and grateful to be a conduit of the innumerable intuitive messages coming through the collective field of consciousness.

To all the words written and spoken throughout the lifetimes of my soul, which elevated my frequency and awareness – I am so grateful and continue to be open to receive.

# PRIMARY SOURCES

Alexander, Eben. *Proof of Heaven: A Neurosurgeon's Journey into the Afterlife.* Simon & Schuster, 2012.

Baker, Ian. *The Heart of the World: A Journey to the Last Sacred Place.* The Penguin Press, 2004.

Barks, Coleman, translator, with John Moyne. *The Essential Rumi.* HarperOne, 2004.

Brach, Tara. *True Refuge: Finding Peace and Freedom in Your Own Awakened Heart.* Bantam, 2013.

Campbell, Joseph. *The Hero with a Thousand Faces.* New World Library, Third Edition, 2008.

Castaneda, Carlos. *The Art of Dreaming.* HarperCollins, 1994.

Chödrön, Pema. *Comfortable with Uncertainty: 108 Teachings on Cultivating Fearlessness and Compassion.* Shambhala, 2002.

Coelho, Paulo. *The Alchemist.* HarperOne, Anniversary Edition, 2014.

Douglas-Klotz, Neil, translator. *Prayers of the Cosmos.* HarperOne, Reprint Edition, 2009.

Freke, Timothy, and Peter Gandy. *The Hermetica: The Lost Wisdom of the Pharaohs.* TarcherPerigee, 1999.

Gilbert, Elizabeth. *Eat, Pray, Love: One Woman's Search for Everything Across Italy, India and Indonesia.* Penguin, 2006.

Greene, Brian. *The Elegant Universe: Superstrings, Hidden Dimensions, and the Quest for the Ultimate Theory*. W. W. Norton & Company, 1999.

Harari, Yuval Noah. *Sapiens: A Brief History of Humankind*. Harper Perennial, 2015.

Harris, Lee, and Diana Edwards. *Awaken Your Multidimensional Soul: Conversations with the Zs: Book Two, Audiobook*. Lee Harris Energy, 2023.

Hartranft, Chip, translator. *The Yoga Sutra of Patanjali*. Shambhala, 2003.

His Holiness the Dalai Lama. *Essence of the Heart Sutra: The Dalai Lama's Heart of Wisdom Teachings*. Translated by Geshe Thupten Jinpa, Wisdom Publications, 2005.

His Holiness the Dalai Lama, and Archbishop Desmond Tutu, with Douglas Abrams. *The Book of Joy: Lasting Happiness in a Changing World*. Avery, 2016.

Homer. *The Odyssey*. Translated by Richmond Lattimore, Harper Perennial, 1999.

Meyer, Marvin. *The Gnostic Gospels of Jesus: The Definitive Collection of Mystical Gospels and Secret Books about Jesus of Nazareth*. HarperSanFrancisco, 2005.

Miller, Donald. *Through Painted Deserts: Light, God, and Beauty on the Open Road*. Harper Horizon, 2005.

Myss, Caroline. *Anatomy of the Spirit: The Seven Stages of Power and Healing*. Harmony Books, 2017.

Oliver, Mary. *A Thousand Mornings*. Penguin Books, 2012.

Peterson, Eugene H. *The Message: The New Testament Psalms and Proverbs*. NavPress, 1995.

Rea, Shiva, *Tending the Heart Fire, Living in Flow with the Pulse of Life*. Sounds True, 2014.

Roche, Lorin. *The Radiance Sutras: 112 Gateways to the Yoga of Wonder and Delight (English and Sanskrit Edition)*. Sounds True, 2014.

Ruiz, Don Miguel. *The Four Agreements: A Practical Guide to Personal Freedom (A Toltec Wisdom Book)*. Amber-Allen, 1997.

Stiene, Frans. *The Inner Heart of Reiki: Rediscovering Your True Self*. Ayni Books, 2015.

Tadd, Ellen. *The Infinite View*. TarcherPerigee, 2017.

Tyson, Neil deGrasse. *Astrophysics for People in a Hurry*. W.W. Norton & Company, 2017.

Wangyal Rinpoche, Tenzin. *Healing with Form, Energy, and Light: The Five Elements in Tibetan Shamanism, Tantra and Dzogchen*. Snow Lion, 2002.

Wallis, Glenn, translator. *The Basic Teachings of the Buddha*. Modern Library, 2007.

Watts, Alan. *Psychotherapy East & West*. New World Library, 1989.

Wilber, Ken. *Integral Meditation*. Shambhala, 2016.

The Bible. Various editions.

# ABOUT THE AUTHOR

Victoria R.G. Newburn, known as Tori, is a seeker, artist, mystic, and intuitive energy guide dedicated to nurturing individual evolution and spiritual growth. She holds an MFA from American University and a BA from DePauw University, along with advanced certifications in Yoga, Meditation, and Astrology. With a deep passion for global religions, mythology, philosophy, science, art, and culture, Tori weaves these influences into her work. From her Indiana homestead, she runs *This Gentle Way*, an online sanctuary offering sacred guidance through retreats, courses, and one-on-one mentorship. Discover more at **thisgentleway.com.**

www.ingramcontent.com/pod-product-compliance
Lightning Source LLC
Chambersburg PA
CBHW021137130626
46554CB00005B/1543